SpringerBriefs in Population Studies

Population Studies of Japan

The world population is expected to expand by 39.4 % to 9.6 billion in 2060 (UN World Population Prospects, revised 2010). Meanwhile, Japan is expected to see its population contract by nearly one-third to 86.7 million, and its proportion of the elderly (65 years of age and over) will account for no less than 39.9 % (National Institute of Population and Social Security Research in Japan, Population Projections for Japan 2012). Japan has entered the post-demographic transitional phase and will be the fastest shrinking country in the world, followed by former Eastern bloc nations, leading other Asian countries that are experiencing drastic changes.

A declining population that is rapidly aging impacts a country's economic growth, labor market, pensions, taxation, health care, and housing. The social structure and geographical distribution in the country will drastically change, and short-term as well as long-term solutions for economic and social consequences of this trend will be required.

This series aims to draw attention to Japan's entering the post-demographic transition phase and to present cutting-edge research in Japanese population studies. It will include compact monographs under the editorial supervision of the Population Association of Japan (PAJ).

The PAJ was established in 1948 and organizes researchers with a wide range of interests in population studies of Japan. The major fields are (1) population structure and aging; (2) migration, urbanization, and distribution; (3) fertility; (4) mortality and morbidity; (5) nuptiality, family, and households; (6) labor force and unemployment; (7) population projection and population policy (including family planning); and (8) historical demography. Since 1978, the PAJ has been publishing the academic journal *Jinkogaku Kenkyu* (The Journal of Population Studies), in which most of the articles are written in Japanese.

Thus, the scope of this series spans the entire field of population issues in Japan, impacts on socioeconomic change, and implications for policy measures. It includes population aging, fertility and family formation, household structures, population health, mortality, human geography and regional population, and comparative studies with other countries.

This series will be of great interest to a wide range of researchers in other countries confronting a post-demographic transition stage, demographers, population geographers, sociologists, economists, political scientists, health researchers, and practitioners across a broad spectrum of social sciences.

More information about this series at http://www.springer.com/series/13101

Shoko Konishi · Emi Tamaki
Jun Yoshinaga

Biodemography of Fertility in Japan

Springer

Shoko Konishi
Department of Human Ecology, School of International Health, Graduate School of Medicine
The University of Tokyo
Tokyo
Japan

and

Department of Anthropology
University of Washington
Seattle, WA
USA

Emi Tamaki
Faculty of International Social Sciences
Gakushuin University
Tokyo
Japan

Jun Yoshinaga
Faculty of Life Sciences
Toyo University
Gunma
Japan

ISSN 2211-3215 ISSN 2211-3223 (electronic)
SpringerBriefs in Population Studies
ISSN 2198-2724 ISSN 2198-2732 (electronic)
Population Studies of Japan
ISBN 978-981-10-0175-8 ISBN 978-981-10-0176-5 (eBook)
https://doi.org/10.1007/978-981-10-0176-5

Library of Congress Control Number: 2017959150

Printed on acid-free paper

This Springer imprint is published by Springer Nature
The registered company is Springer Nature Singapore Pte Ltd.
The registered company address is: 152 Beach Road, #21-01/04 Gateway East, Singapore 189721, Singapore

Preface

Why are Japanese people having fewer children? Why is human fertility decreasing in many parts of the global population? These questions are simple but nonetheless quite difficult to answer. Research in Japan and other countries suggests, albeit indirectly, that low fertility is not merely the consequence of people's choices but also the result of biological inability to have a child regardless of a couple's desire. In other words, in addition to social and cultural factors that induce people to choose not to have (any more) children, biological/physiological factors (e.g., increases in infertility) may play important roles in fertility trends.

When couples start childbearing later in life (which is especially prevalent in recent years), their fecundity (the biological ability to conceive) is expected to be lower than that of couples who start childbearing when younger. It is suspected that the reproductive aging of couples trying to conceive leads to increased infertility, which is linked to low fertility. In addition to this secular change in childbearing ages, which has been observed in many countries in the world, we suspect that social and cultural factors peculiar to Japan may play a role in the trend toward low fertility in this setting.

Social, cultural, and biological factors interrelate to form fertility trends. Using a proximate determinants concept, we can decompose fertility into biobehavioral factors that are related to sociocultural factors. This decomposition of fertility is useful when trying to understand the mechanisms of fertility trends. Among the list of proximate determinants proposed by James W. Wood (i.e., age at marriage or entry into sexual union, age at menarche, age at menopause, age at onset of pathological sterility, duration of lactational infecundability, duration of the fecund waiting time to conception, probability of fetal loss, length of the nonsusceptible period associated with each fetal loss, and length of gestation resulting in live birth), we place particular emphasis on two components—duration of fecund waiting time to conception and duration of lactational infecundability—as well as their subcomponents. These two components are related to both biological and cultural factors and show significant between- and within-population variations. By focusing on these two variables, we hope to understand the characteristics of fertility trends that are either unique to Japan or common across Japan and other settings.

The primary objective of this book is to present our original data regarding the fertility of Japanese population based on the concepts of proximate determinants of fertility. We also focus on similarities and differences in proximate determinants of fertility between couples in Japan and in other settings. By contrasting our results with data from other countries, we intend to provide a deeper understanding of how Japanese fertility is affected by various components.

The first chapter (by Konishi and Tamaki) summarizes the theoretical model of proximate determinants of fertility and introduces the terminology that will be used in this book. It also describes what is currently known about the social and biomedical background of low fertility in Japan. In the second chapter (by Konishi and Tamaki), we report original data collected in the biodemography project conducted in Japan in 2014 by Konishi and Tamaki. In addition, we include a review of previous studies on factors related to time to pregnancy (TTP) and lactational infecundability that target populations in Japan and overseas. Data from the biodemography project and a review of previous studies (Chap. 2) demonstrate that duration of lactational infecundability and TTP may be longer among Japanese couples than among those in Western settings. The longer TTP of Japanese couples may be linked to low coital frequency and possibly to menstrual cycle alterations, which are related to social factors such as prolonged working hours and the preference for thinness. The third chapter (by Yoshinaga) summarizes previous studies on a possible association between chemical exposure and TTP and presents original Japanese data from Yoshinaga and colleagues on this topic. Considering that previous studies report—albeit inconsistently—an impact of environmental exposure on TTP and that there are massive numbers of chemical substances surrounding the contemporary populations, it is possible that within-couple variations in TTP can be partly explained by couples' exposure to various substances. Finally, in the last chapter (by Konishi, Tamaki, and Yoshinaga), we propose future research topics to better understand mechanisms of fertility changes in Japan. We believe it will help us to obtain more detailed answers to the following question: Why do low fertility levels persist in many parts of the global population?

Lastly, we thank Dr. Kathleen A. O'Connor, Dr. Masahiro Umezaki, and a reviewer who read the earlier draft of this book and gave critical comments.

Tokyo, Japan Shoko Konishi
Tokyo, Japan Emi Tamaki
Gunma, Japan Jun Yoshinaga

Contents

Chapter 1
Introduction

Shoko Konishi and Emi Tamaki

Abstract Human fertility (measured by total fertility rate, TFR) varies widely even among populations without any artificial fertility control, whereas the age pattern of fertility is similar across populations. Proximate determinants of fertility are useful tools for understanding why fertility varies across populations and ages in general. In this chapter, we argue that Wood's proximate determinants of fertility are useful in decomposing the mechanisms of low fertility in Japan, and we provide definitions of the terminology used in this book, such as fertility, fecundity, fecundability, and infertility. Social characteristics interact with biology to form fertility trend. For example, the increasing age at marriage and childbearing is suspected to reduce fertility by lengthening fecund waiting time to conception and increasing the probability of fetal loss, both of which are proximate determinants affected by reproductive aging. Social norm characteristics in Japan, such as long working hours, can also lengthen fecund waiting time to conception, likely through decreased frequency of sexual intercourse and increased probability of anovulatory menstrual cycles. Other factors may also influence these and other proximate determinants, including reproductive aging, assisted reproductive technology (ART), and environmental chemicals, although less is known about how these other factors may influence individual- and population-level fertility measures.

Keywords Fecundability · Fecundity · Fertility · Infertility · Proximate determinants · Biodemography · Japan · TFR

1.1 Heterogeneous Fertility Across Populations and Ages

Human fertility varies widely across populations. The highest TFR in 2015 was found in Niger (7.6), and the lowest TFR, 1.2, was observed in countries such as Bosnia-Herzegovina, South Korea, Portugal, and Taiwan [1]. Although the use of modern contraceptives plays an important role in the observed variations in fertility, there are large interpopulation differences in fertility even without modern contraception.

S. Konishi et al., *Biodemography of Fertility in Japan*,
Population Studies of Japan, https://doi.org/10.1007/978-981-10-0176-5_1

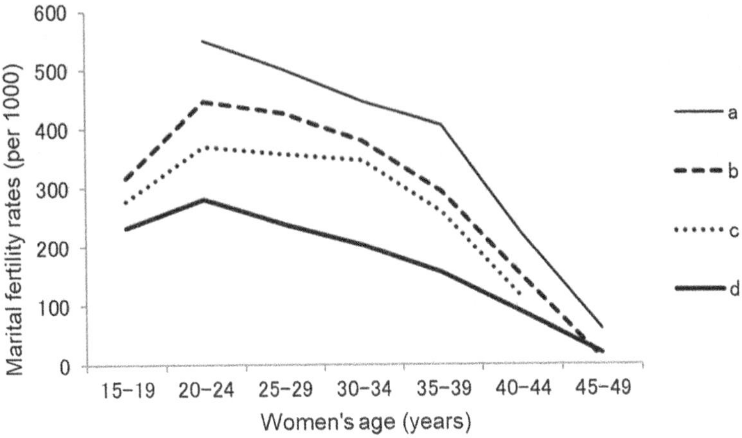

Fig. 1.1 Age-specific marital fertility rate (ASMFR) of natural fertility populations. **a** Hutterites in the USA, marriages in 1921–1930; **b** Northwest France, marriages in 1670–1769; **c** Punjab Chamars villages, women born in 1900–1914; and **d** Mino agricultural area in Japan, women born in 1651–1825 *Data source* **a**, **b**, **c**: [37], **d**: [38]

In natural fertility populations where modern contraceptives are not used, fertility varied significantly across populations. Such variations in fertility persist even after the effect of age at marriage is controlled for. In fact, the age-specific marital fertility (ASMFR) differs widely across natural fertility populations (Fig. 1.1). In contrast, the age pattern of ASMFR (i.e., being highest in a woman's early twenties and then decreasing she ages) is similar across populations. This age pattern is believed to be strongly linked to reproductive aging of both women and men, which may act through decreased frequency of sexual intercourse, the probability of conception, increased probability of fetal loss, and/or other factors [2].

To understand the underlying mechanisms of such variations in fertility across ages and/or across populations, the concept of proximate determinants is useful.

1.2 Terminology

1.2.1 Definitions of Terminology Related to Fertility

Before engaging in a detailed discussion of proximate determinants of fertility, it would be useful to summarize the terminology that will be used in this book. The word fertility is used in different ways in the medical literature and in social sciences, such as the field of demography. In the medical literature, the word fertility often refers to the biological ability to produce, whereas in the field of demography, fertility refers to the number of children actually born [2] (p. 3). In this book, we adopt Wood's definitions for these terms. According to Wood [2], fertility refers to the production of a live birth and fecundity refers to the biological ability to produce. Fecundability is the probability that a fecund couple will conceive during a month of exposure to unprotected intercourse [2] (p. 72). Time to pregnancy (TTP), or waiting time to conception [3], refers to the number of months (or menstrual cycles) that a couple requires to conceive, which can alternatively be defined as the length of time between discontinuing contraception and conception. More specifically, Wood uses the term "fecund waiting time to conception", which "refers to the lag between a woman's entrance into the fecund state (in which she is potentially able to conceive) and her next conception" (p. 72) [2].

1.2.2 Definitions of Infertility

Like the word fertility, the term infertility has several definitions. In this book, we define infertility as a status in which a couple (or a woman) does not conceive while using no contraceptive, regardless of the frequency of intercourse or pregnancy intention. Exclusion of coital frequency from the definition contrasts with clinical definitions, which will be outlined below. Our definition is fairly close to Wood's definition of infertility, which is described simply as "the nonproduction of a live birth" (p. 444) [2]. Infertility can be caused by sterility, the actual physiological inability to produce a live birth (p. 445) [2], or by other factors, such as low (or no) fecundability or low (or no) coital frequency.

Clinical definitions of infertility often require the occurrence of regular unprotected intercourse. For example, the Japan Society of Obstetrics and Gynecology defines infertility as the "inability to conceive within 1 year while having intercourse without contraception and wanting to become pregnant" [4] (translated by authors). Similarly, the World Health Organization (WHO) defines infertility as "a disease of the reproductive system defined by the failure to achieve a clinical pregnancy after 12 months or more of regular unprotected sexual intercourse" [5]. The Centers for Disease Control and Prevention (CDC) of the USA defines infertility as "not being able to get pregnant (conceive) after one year of unprotected sex" [6].

Whereas these current definitions of infertility all include a one-year cutoff, the duration for judging a couple infertile has changed in the past several decades. For example, a Japanese Encyclopedia of Obstetrics and Gynecology published in 1956 [7] (pp. 2–5) reports that different researchers in Japan and in other countries recommend different cutoffs, i.e., 2, 3, 4, or 5 years. Furthermore, Yuzuki [7] wrote that although shorter cutoffs can facilitate medical treatment for infertility, it can also produce more false positives and may cause some couples who are able to conceive naturally to be deemed infertile. He argued that to obtain an appropriate cutoff, it is necessary to examine statistical data from Japanese populations regarding how many newly married women conceive by the end of each year after marriage. After reviewing previous studies, he concluded that 3 years would be a suitable cutoff for collecting epidemiological information on infertility, whereas a clinical cutoff of

2 years would be preferable for purposes of considering medical treatment. More recently, in 2015, the Japan Society of Obstetrics and Gynecology changed the cutoff for infertility from the typical 2 years (1–3 years) to 1 year, because "institutions abroad (WHO, ICMART, ASMR, ESHRE[1]) define infertility with a 1-year cutoff" [8] (translated by authors).

The number of couples in Japan who currently fall within the criteria of infertility is unknown, and thus, the increase in the number of infertility cases due to the reduced cutoff period is also unknown.

1.3 Proximate Determinants of Fertility

Proximate determinants are variables that have a direct effect on fertility. Any factor that potentially affects reproduction acts through one or more proximate determinants. The proximate determinants approach was first developed by Davis and Blake [9] and then modified by John Bongaarts and others [10–12]. Wood [2] further refined the list of proximate determinants, placing more emphasis on biobehavioral factors. Wood's proximate determinants of natural fertility (Table 1.1) do not include contraception or induced abortion, both of which were on Bongaarts' list of proximate determinants; however, Wood's list can be applied to populations with controlled fertility, because any form of contraception can work by affecting one or more proximate determinants. For example, induced abortion can be viewed as an artificial modification of the probability of fetal loss. Oral contraceptive pills reduce the proportion of ovulatory cycles to zero; barrier methods such as condoms can reduce the frequency of insemination by preventing semen from entering the vagina. We conclude that Wood's list of proximate determinants of natural fertility (Table 1.1) is useful in understanding the mechanisms of low fertility in contemporary populations, including the population of Japan, by decomposing fertility into biobehavioral factors.

In this book, we basically adopt Wood's list of proximate determinants (Table 1.1), which includes age at marriage or entry into sexual union, age at menarche, age at menopause, age at onset of pathological sterility, duration of lactational infecundability, duration of the fecund waiting time to conception, probability of fetal loss, length of the nonsusceptible period associated with each fetal loss, and length of gestation resulting in live birth. We place particular emphasis on two of the proximate determinants, i.e., duration of postpartum amenorrhea and fecund waiting time to conception, anticipating that their possible impacts on TFR are large and that their between- and within-population variations are substantial because they reflect both biological and cultural differences.

[1]WHO: World Health Organization; ICMART: The International Committee Monitoring Assisted Reproductive Technologies; ASMR: American Society for Reproductive Medicine; and ESHRE: European Society of Human Reproduction and Embryology.

Table 1.1 The proximate determinants of natural fertility [2]

I. Exposure factors
*1. Age at marriage or entry into sexual union
2. Age at menarche
3. Age at menopause
4. Age at onset of pathological sterility (if earlier than menopause)
II. Susceptibility factors
**5. Duration of lactational infecundability
**6. Duration of the fecund waiting time to conception (determined by the following fecundability factors)
**6.1. frequency of insemination
6.2. length of ovarian cycles
6.3. proportion of ovulatory cycles
6.4. duration of the fertility period, given ovulation[a]
6.5. probability of conception from a single insemination in the fertile period
*7. Probability of fetal loss[b]
8. Length of the nonsusceptible period associated with each fetal loss[c]
9. Length of gestation resulting in live birth

Factors with asterisks are reviewed in this book, with particular emphasis on factors with two asterisks

[a]The fertility period is the mid-portion of the cycle when insemination has some nonzero probability of resulting in conception

[b]Following World Health Organization recommendations [36], fetal loss refers to all spontaneous abortions and thus includes both miscarriages and stillbirths

[c]The nonsusceptible period associated with a fetal loss includes truncated gestations ending in loss plus any residual period of infecundability following the loss

According to Wood's sensitivity analysis [2] (pp. 514–515), these factors are known to contribute to between-population variations in TFR among natural fertility populations. We review previous studies targeting populations in Japan that consider factors that are directly or indirectly related to these two proximate determinants. By referring to several previous studies targeting overseas populations, we focus on possible differences and similarities between populations in Japan and those in other countries. We believe that these data will be useful in understanding the mechanisms of fertility trends in this setting.

There are several components of the proximate determinants of fertility that are not mentioned in this book. Length of the nonsusceptible period associated with each fetal loss and length of gestation resulting in live birth are not discussed in this book because between-population variations of these factors are thought to be small and thus unlikely to explain variations in fertility. We believe that age at menarche plays only a minor role in fertility trends in Japan and in many other countries where women start sexual relationships and reproduction years after menarche. Age at menopause or age at the onset of pathological sterility may have some impact on fertility trends, especially when couples start childbearing at higher ages. However, we do not include these factors in this book because their effects are indirectly reflected in prolonged TTP. Theoretically, sterility and reduced fecundity (due to either natural aging or pathological causes) differ from each other, but it is difficult to distinguish them in an empirical epidemiological study. In other words, if a couple waits a long time to conceive, it is often difficult to tell whether they are sterile or have reduced fecundity. Therefore, we focus only on TTP. Prolonged TTP in older couples can be understood as reflecting sterility or reduced fecundity due to reproductive aging and/or pathological causes.

1.4 Biodemography of Fertility

There are numerous definitions and branches of biodemography that target both fertility and mortality [13]. In the present book, we define biodemography of fertility simply as an approach to decompose fertility into its proximate determinants [14].

A paper by Kono [14] titled "A bio-demographic analysis of Japanese fertility via micro-simulation" was published in 1984. The purposes of the paper were to decompose Japanese fertility into proximate determinants and to assess the possible impact of changes in certain fertility variables using a simulation approach. The author acknowledged that to identify socioeconomic determinants affecting levels and trends of fertility, it is necessary to study the relationships between fertility and the proximate determinants. Although the importance of proximate determinants was acknowledged as early as the 1980s and micro-simulation models have been proposed [14, 15], research that empirically quantifies these factors and/or estimates the possible impact of the proximate determinants of fertility in the Japanese population remains limited. Nonetheless, we believe that the biodemographic framework can be useful for studying the contemporary population of Japan, where the age at childbearing continues to rise and it is suspected that an increasing number of couples are unable to have children despite a desire for them [16].

Although we follow their definitions and framework of the biodemography of fertility, we expand the biodemographic framework to include the possible effects of environmental exposure and infertility treatments, two variables that have received more attention in recent years. As summarized in Chap. 3, chemical exposure in daily life (i.e., not occupational exposure) might have some impact on fecundity (the biological ability to produce). Although several epidemiologic and animal studies have reported possible negative effects on fecundity, it is unknown what impact chemical exposure might have on fertility (the number of children actually born). Using the biodemographic approach, we will be able to estimate the possible effect of chemical exposure on human fertility. Infertility treatments are becoming more common for couples who desire children but do not get pregnant within a certain time frame despite their efforts to do so. Although clinical data on infertility treatments have been accumulated, their potential impact on fertility has not been well investigated, an issue that will be further discussed in Chap. 2.

1.5 Social Background of Low Fertility in Japan

In this section, we illuminate social factors (Fig. 1.2) related to the decline of fertility in postwar Japan. In particular, we consider how these factors could influence fertility through the proximate determinants suggested by Wood [2].

We start with the age at marriage and entry into sexual union, two components in Wood's exposure factors (see Table 1.1). Over the last half-century, the average age of first marriage for women in Japan has increased from 23.0 years in 1950 to 28.8 years in 2010 [17]. Because out-of-wedlock childbearing is rare in Japan (approximately 1–2% [17]), the average age of first childbearing has also increased, from 25.1 years in 1955 to 29.3 years in 2010 [18]. At the population level, the postponement of marriage and childbearing has led to a decline in TFR per woman from 3.7 in 1950 to 1.3 in 2005 [17], making the Japanese fertility rate one of the lowest in the world. Figure 1.3 shows the 5-year age-specific fertility rates of Japanese women in 1950, 1970, 1990, and 2010 [19], showing the decline and postponement of childbearing in the past half-century.

Whereas the age at marriage is increasing, data from the Japanese Association for Sex Education indicate that the age at entry into sexual union declined in the 1990s and reached a plateau around 2005 [20]. These data show that the percentage of high school boys who have experienced sexual intercourse increased from 14% in 1992 to 27% in 1999. For high school girls, the rate increased from 16 to 24% in the same time period [20]. According to Sato et al. [21], pregnancy and abortion rates for 15–19-year-old girls also increased between 1975 and 2004, despite the fact that the overall rates declined during the same time period. Another study [22]

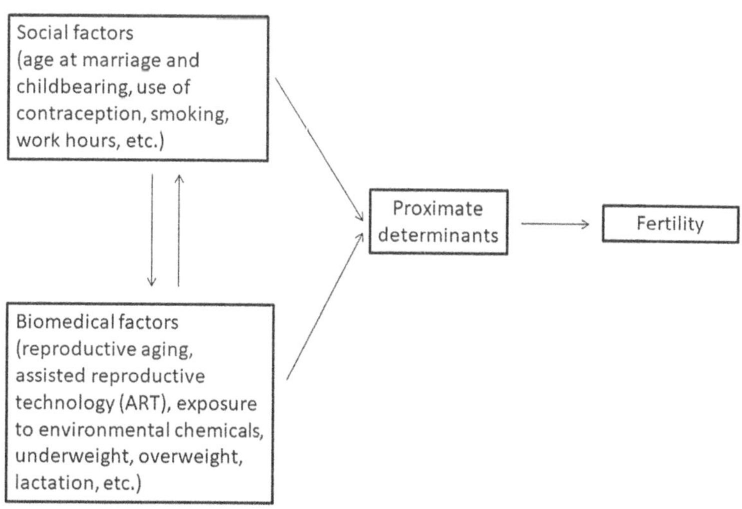

Fig. 1.2 Framework of biodemography of fertility. Both social and biomedical factors affect fertility through proximate determinants

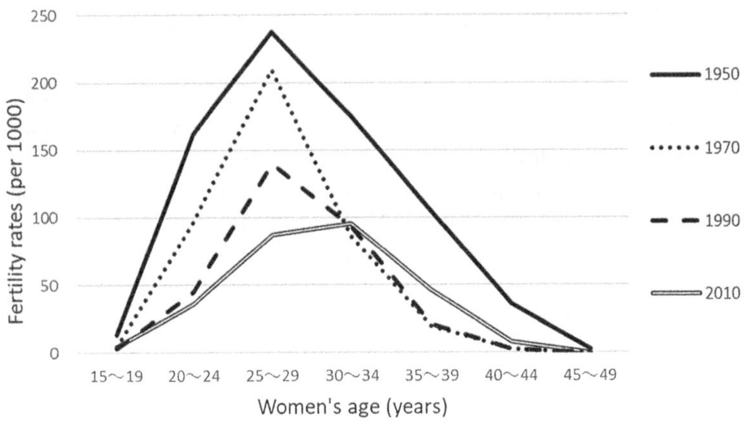

Fig. 1.3 Age-specific fertility rates: Japan, 1950–2010 *Data source* [19]

reports that the percentage of first births among 15–19-year-olds that were conceived before marriage increased from 61.5% in 1985 to 82.9% in 2004, suggesting an underlying rise in sexual activities among people in their late teens. Regardless, the proportion of births attributable to 15–19-year-olds has remained at approximately 1.5% since the mid-1980s[2]; therefore, we suspect that the declining age of entry into sexual union has a minimal impact on TFR.

Several sociocultural explanations for the postponement of marriage and childbearing in Japan have been put forward. Many argue that women's educational attainment and participation in the labor force have contributed to delays in marriage and childbearing. The School Basic Survey shows that women's rate of entry into higher education increased from 32% in 1975 to 57% in 2016 [23]. Women's entrance into the paid labor force has also increased, especially among young women. The female labor force participation rate among 25–29-year-old women increased from 50.1% in 1950 to 72.4% in 2010 [24]. According to several studies, Japanese women's economic independence combined with men's increasing economic instability has most likely led them to delay marriage and parenthood until a suitable partner can be found [25, 26]. In addition to changes in women's status, work–family incompatibility is considered to encourage postponement of childbearing in modern Japan. The lack of affordable childcare, long work hours, and the cost of raising children can potentially reduce a couple's willingness to have children. The postponement of childbearing is in turn likely to affect susceptibility factors, especially the duration of the fecund waiting time to conceive and the probability of fetal loss due to aging (see Sect. 1.6 for details).

Cultural norms surrounding contraception are also likely to shape Japanese fertility trends through proximate determinants. Unreliable methods, such as condoms and withdrawal, are common in Japan [27], which may result in unintended

[2]Calculated by authors using data from NIPSSR [40].

pregnancies by inadvertently increasing the frequency of insemination. The Ministry of Health, Labour and Welfare [28] calculates that one in four first births in 2009 was conceived before marriage. In addition, abortion is legal under certain conditions, including economic and health reasons. It is possible that abortion may in some cases be used as a backup for failed (or a lack of reliable) birth control. According to the survey conducted by the Mainichi newspaper, approximately 18% of women aged 20–24 years indicated that if their contraception failed, they would consider an artificial abortion [27].

Finally, we argue that the work conditions that characterize Japanese society, such as long work hours and job stress associated with overwork, may impact fertility through the proportion of ovulatory cycles, frequency of insemination, and probability of fetal loss. Several studies have found that women with high job stress and long work hours are more likely to have irregular and shorter menstrual cycles [29, 30], which have been linked in several other studies to anovulation and longer waiting time to conceive [31]. Regarding the frequency of insemination, Genda and Kawakami [32] found that long work hours are associated with lower coital frequencies among married salaried workers in Japan. Furthermore, long working hours in general are linked to spontaneous abortions [33], although the effect is small. Fenster and others [34] found an association between job stress and spontaneous abortion in the presence of other risk factors, such as smoking. Taken together, although there is limited evidence from Japan, these studies suggest that the Japanese work environment may in some cases compromise fertility through several biological pathways.

1.6 Biomedical Background of Low Fertility in Japan

In general, it is expected that biomedical factors such as reproductive aging, assisted reproductive technology (ART), and exposure to environmental chemicals have impacts on proximate determinants of fertility and thus on fertility (Fig. 1.2).

Reproductive aging may affect fertility by lengthening TTP, which can be further decomposed into factors such as reduced frequency of ovulation, reduced frequency of sexual intercourse, reduced probability of conception per insemination, and increased fetal loss. Reproductive aging of men might also be associated with reduced frequency of sexual intercourse and reduced probability of conception per insemination. By decomposing the effect of reproductive aging on fertility into each component, we could help to explore how to overcome the negative impact of aging more efficiently in terms of fertility.

Reproductive aging may have demographic consequences, such as higher rates of nulliparity. Supporting this notion, a higher age of women at first marriage is strongly associated with a higher probability of nulliparity at age 40 after adjusting for possible confounders [35]. The data imply that reproductive aging of women contributes to the increasing number of couples who are unable to have children despite wanting them, i.e., by lengthening the time to successful pregnancy. It is expected that the impact of reproductive aging on fertility is increasing in Japan because the number of women of reproductive age (18–49 years old) who intend to have a (an additional) child increased from 9.78 million in 1982 to 11.47 million in 2005, and the 17% increase was accompanied by aging; specifically, the proportion of women 35 years and older increased from 5 to 15% in same time period [16].

Because many couples are unable to conceive naturally due to reproductive aging and/or other reasons, a substantial proportion of these Japanese couples have received infertility treatments in recent years. Childbirths resulting from ART (defined as in vitro fertilization, micro-insemination, or frozen embryo transfer) accounted for 3.7% of all births in the country in 2012 [36]. Hayashi [36] estimated that the TFR of 1.41 in 2012 would have decreased to 1.36 if no ART had been performed. However, we should note that numerous other treatment cycles failed to produce live births. The demographic and sociocultural consequences of such massive use of infertility treatment must be evaluated carefully and will be further discussed in Chap. 2.

In addition to reproductive aging and infertility treatment, there is concern about the possible detrimental effects of environmental chemicals on human reproduction, as will be summarized in Chap. 3. Although the debate continues, a number of studies suggest that exposure to certain environmental chemicals is associated with decreased fecundity as measured by prolonged TTP. The effect of environmental chemical exposure on TTP will be reviewed and discussed in detail in Chap. 3.

References

1. Population Reference Bureau. 2015. *2015 World Population Data Sheet*. Washington, DC.
2. Wood, James W. 1994. *Dynamics of human reproduction: biology, biometry, demography*. New York: Aldine de Gruyter.
3. Baird, Donna Day, Allen J. Wilcox, and Clarice R. Weinberg. 1986. Use of time to pregnancy to study environmental exposures. *American Journal of Epidemiology* 124: 470–480.
4. Japan Society of Obstetrics and Gynecology. 2016. Infertility (funin). http://www.jsog.or.jp/public/knowledge/funin.html. Accessed 15 Dec. (in Japanese).
5. Sullivan, E.A., F. Zegers-Hochschild, R. Mansour, O. Ishihara, J. De Mouzon, K.G. Nygren, and G.D. Adamson. 2013. International committee for monitoring assisted reproductive technologies (ICMART) world report: Assisted reproductive technology 2004. *Human Reproduction* 28: 1375–1390.
6. Centers for Disease Control and Prevention. 2016. Infertility|Reproductive Health|CDC. https://www.cdc.gov/reproductivehealth/infertility/. Accessed 15 Dec.
7. Yuzuki, Shozaburo. 1956. Definitions of infertility. *Japanese Encyclopedia of Obstetrics and Gynecology (Nippon sanka fujinka zensho)*. (in Japanese).
8. Japan Society of Obstetrics and Gynecology. 2016. Change of the definition of infertility (Funin no teigi no henko nitsuite). http://www.jsog.or.jp/news/html/announce_20150902.html . Accessed 15 Dec 2016. (in Japanese).
9. Davis, Kingsley, and Judith Blake. 1956. Social structure and fertility: An analytic framework. *Economic Development and Cultural Change* 4: 211–235.
10. Bongaarts, John. 1978. A framework for analyzing the proximate determinants of fertility. *Population and Development Review* 4: 105–132.

11. Bongaarts, John. 1976. Intermediate fertility variables and marital fertility rates. *Population Studies* 30: 227–241.
12. Bongaarts, J. 1982. The fertility-inhibiting effects of the intermediate fertility variables. *Studies in Family Planning* 13: 179–189.
13. Carey, James R, and James W. Vaupel. 2006. Biodemography. In *Handbook of population*, 625–658.
14. Kono, Shigemi. 1984. A bio-demographic analysis of the Japanese fertility via micro-simulation. *Journal of Population Studies* 7: 24–32.
15. Institute of Population Problems. 1984. *Biodemographic analysis offertility (shusshoryoku no seibutsujinkogakuteki bunseki)*. (in Japanese).
16. Iwasawa, Miho, and Fusami Mita. 2007. Delayed childbearing and the changing age composition of women who desire children (Bansanka to Kyojikibo josei jinkou no koreika). *Journal of Population Problems* 63: 24–41. (in Japanese).
17. National Institute of Population and Social Security Research. 2016. *Latest demographic statistics*. Tokyo: National Institute of Population and Social Security Research. (in Japanese).
18. National Institute of Population and Social Security Research. 2012. *Latest demographic statistics*. Tokyo: National Institute of Population and Social Security Research. (in Japanese).
19. Hara, Junsuke, and Kazuo Katase. 2012. Summary of 7th national survey on adolescent sexual behaviors (2011) (Dai 7 kai seishounen no seikoudou zenkokuchosa (2011nen) no gaiyo). *Modern Sex Education Research Journal (Gendai seikyoiku kenkyu janaru)* 17: 1–18. (in Japanese).
20. Sato, Ryuzaburo, Noriko Shiraishi, and Rieko Bando. 2008. Induced abortion in Japan: A demographic analysis of its trends and causes. National Institute of Population and Social Science Research Working Paper No. 22.
21. Ministry of Health Labour and Welfare. 2005. *Live Births: Special Report of Vital Statistics 2005*. (in Japanese).
22. Ministry of Education Culture Sports Science and Technology. 2016. Education continuance rate. *School Basic Survey*. (in Japanese).
23. National Institute of Population and Social Security Research. 2015. *Latest demographic statistics*. Tokyo: National Institute of Population and Social Security Research. (in Japanese).
24. Kono, Shigemi. 2007. *Invitation to demography (Jinkogaku eno shotai)*. Tokyo: Chuokoronshinsha. (in Japanese).
25. Tsutsui, Junya. 2015. *Work and family (Shigoto to Kazoku)*. Tokyo: Chuokoronshinsha. (in Japanese).
26. Hayashi, Kenji. 2005. Sex, pregnancy and childbearing behaviors and traditions among contemporary women (Gendaijosei no sei to ninnshinn/shussann no kodo oyobi sono densho nitsuite). In *Family attitudes in an era of very low fertility: Report on the first national survey on population, family and generations in Japan (Choshoshika jikai no kazokuishiki)*, ed. Mainichi Shimbun Population Problems Research Council, 195–214. Tokyo: Mainichi Newspaper. (in Japanese).
27. Ministry of Health Labour and Welfare. 2010. *Live Births: Special Report of Vital Statistics 2010.*
28. Fenster, L., K. Waller, J. Chen, A.E. Hubbard, G.C. Windham, E. Elkin, and S. Swan. 1999. Psychological stress in the workplace and menstrual function. *American Journal of Epidemiology* 149: 127–134.
29. Lawson, Christina C., Candice Y. Johnson, Jorge E. Chavarro, Eileen N. Lividoti, Elizabeth A. Hibert, Carissa M. Whelan, Barbara Grajewski Rocheleau, Eva S. Schernhammer, and Janet W. Rich-Edwards. 2015. Work schedule and physically demanding work in relation to menstrual function: The nurses' health study 3. *Scandinavian Journal of Work, Environment & Health* 41: 194–203.
30. Wise, Lauren A., Ellen M. Mikkelsen, Kenneth J. Rothman, Anders H. Riis, Henrik Toft Sørensen, Krista F. Huybrechts, and Elizabeth E. Hatch. 2011. A prospective cohort study of menstrual characteristics and time to pregnancy. *American Journal of Epidemiology* 174: 701–709.

31. Genda, Yuji, and Atsushi Kawakami. 2006. Employment polarization and sexual behavior (Shugyo nikyokuka to seikodo). *The Japanese Journal of Labour Studies* 556: 80–91. (in Japanese).
32. Bonde, Jens Peter, Kristian Tore Jørgensen, Matteo Bonzini, and Keith T. Palmer. 2013. Miscarriage and occupational activity: A systematic review and meta-analysis regarding shift work, working hours, lifting, standing, and physical workload. *Scandinavian Journal of Work, Environment & Health* 39: 325–334.
33. Fenster, Laura, Catherine Schaefer, Ashwini Mathur, Robert A. Hiatt, Carl Pieper, Alan E. Hubbard, Julie Von Behren, and Shanna H. Swan. 1995. Psychologic stress in the workplace and spontaneous abortion. *American Journal of Epidemiology* 142: 1176–1183.
34. Suga, Keita. 2008. Patterns and covariates of childless at the age of forty in Japan. *Journal of Population Studies* 42: 57–70. (in Japanese).
35. Hayashi, Reiko. 2015. Demographic impact of assisted reproductive technology (Seishoku hojo iryo no jinkougakuteki inpakuto). *Igakunoayumi* 254: 185–188. (in Japanese).
36. World Health Organization. 1977. Recommended definitions, terminology and format for statistical tables related to the perinatal period and use of a new certificate for cause of perinatal deaths. *Acta Obstetrica et Gynaecologica Scandinavica* 56: 247–253.
37. Leridon, Henri. 1977. *Human fertility: The basic components*. Trans. Judith F. Helzner. Chicago and London: The University of Chicago Press.
38. Hayami, Akira. 1992. *Population, economy and society in early modern Japan (Kinsei nobi chiho no jinko keizai shakai)*. Tokyo: Sobunsha. (in Japanese).
39. National Institute of Population and Social Security Research. 2016. *The fifteenth Japanese National Fertility Survey*. Tokyo: National Institute of Population and Social Security Research. (in Japanese).

Chapter 2
Proximate Determinants of Fertility in Japan

Shoko Konishi and Emi Tamaki

Abstract Proximate determinants link both social and biological factors to fertility. In this section, we will summarize available data related to proximate determinants of fertility in Japan while referring to some of the related literature targeting populations overseas. In addition to data from published studies, we present our original data collected in the biodemography project, an Internet-based cross-sectional survey on reproductive history conducted in 2014 targeting Japanese women between 20 and 44 years of age. Following Wood's conceptualization, the specific components of the proximate determinants of fertility referred to in this chapter are lactational infecundability, fecund waiting time to conception, and fetal loss (both spontaneous and induced). Additionally, papers on factors that are expected to significantly affect fecund waiting time to conception, i.e., frequency of sexual intercourse, length and regularity of menstrual cycle, and use of contraception and infertility treatment, will be reviewed.

Keywords Internet-based survey · Lactational amenorrhea · Menstrual cycle
Time to pregnancy (TTP) · Assisted reproductive technology (ART)
Japan

2.1 Biodemography Project

The biodemography project was an Internet-based survey that targeted women aged 20–44 years old who resided across Japan at the time of survey in 2014 [1]. This project was supported by KAKENHI 70451771 and Ritsumeikan University Institute of Human Sciences, Exploratory Research Fund. The primary purpose of the project was to estimate fecundity and its covariates, including proximate determinants, by applying the current duration approach [2, 3]. The respondents (n = 3214, a 30.7% response rate) were recruited from a group of research participants of a market research company called Intage, Inc.

Based on the rationale presented below, we deem it useful to show certain data from the biodemography project and to propose future research topics that are

S. Konishi et al., *Biodemography of Fertility in Japan*,
Population Studies of Japan, https://doi.org/10.1007/978-981-10-0176-5_2

important to an understanding of the fertility trend in Japan. Internet-based recruitment of and follow-up with participants have been successfully used in recent studies on time to pregnancy (TTP) in Denmark [4] and in the USA [5]. In Japan, numerous research companies provide online research services that focus mainly on business marketing through the distribution of questionnaires to their registered research monitors. Use of the Internet is especially helpful in reaching young people, who are relatively difficult to reach with traditional recruiting methods, such as mailings or visits by researchers. Another benefit of Internet-based surveys is cost-effectiveness [4]. Because the process is much less expensive than paper- or interview-based questionnaire surveys, researchers can target a larger number of individuals compared with traditional methods with the same budget and can conduct a pilot survey before implementing a survey that targets a nationally representative sample. Although the representativeness of the sample of an Internet-based survey is not as definitive as that of a nationally representative sample, Hatch et al. [6] evaluated selection bias in an Internet-based preconception cohort (Snart Gravid $n = 4801$) with data from the Danish medical birth registry and concluded that recruiting reproductive-aged women via the Internet "may be no more prone to selection bias than traditional methods of recruitment." Based on the above-mentioned information, we conclude that an Internet-based survey is useful, especially when asking personal questions that seek information regarding factors such as contraceptive use and sexual behavior, which is hard to obtain from face-to-face or paper-based interview surveys.

We compared the participants of the biodemography project with the population of the entire country of Japan (based on the 2010 Population Census) with respect to the distribution of partnership status by women's ages (Table 2.1). In the younger age-groups, there is a higher proportion of married participants in the biodemography project compared with the national sample. In the older age-groups, the partner status distribution is more or less similar between the two populations, although the "unknown" category is included only in the national sample (in contrast to a paper-based survey, an Internet-based survey can ensure that participants select a response for every question). Basic characteristics of the respondents are summarized in Table 2.2.

2.2 Lactational Infecundability

Lactational infecundability, or postpartum amenorrhea, refers to the time period between the end of pregnancy and resumption of fecundity. In Japan [7] and many other countries [8], prolonged duration of postpartum amenorrhea is consistently found among mothers who breast-feed for longer durations compared with those who breast-feed for shorter durations. It can be hypothesized that the increasing proportion of breastfeeding mothers in Japan contributes to prolonged duration of postpartum amenorrhea, which in turn could be linked to the risk of secondary infertility. Although there is not yet enough data to test this supposition, future

Table 2.1 Age and partnership status of participants in the biodemography project and the total population of Japan [1]

	Biodemography project[a] (n = 3196) (%)				Japan[b] (%)				
	Married	Unmarried, partnered	Unmarried, no partner	Total	Married	Unmarried, partnered	Unmarried, no partner	Unknown	Total
20–24	13	35	52	100	9	34	51	5	100
25–29	49	21	30	100	36	23	36	5	100
30–34	64	14	21	100	60	10	26	5	100
35–39	71	10	19	100	69	5	23	4	100
40–44	73	7	20	100	72	26		2	100
Total	61	14	24	100	52	46		2	100

[a]No participants were in the unknown category

[b]Estimated based on the 2010 Population Census (proportions of married and unmarried) [56] and the National Survey on Fertility 2010 (proportion of women with a partner among unmarried women) [57]. Because no data are available for 40–44-year-old women in the National Survey on Fertility, the proportions of unmarried women with and without male partners could not be calculated for this age-group

Table 2.2 Basic demographic characteristics of participants in the biodemography project (n = 3196)

Characteristics	n	Proportions (%)
Age (year)		
20–24	279	9
25–29	525	16
30–34	715	22
35–39	832	26
40–44	845	26
Education[a]		
High school or less	912	29
Junior college/vocational school	1120	35
University or higher	1164	36
Annual household income (million yen)		
Less than 3	961	30
3–4.9	801	25
5–9.9	800	25
10+	634	20
Partnership status		
Married	1965	61
Unmarried, partnered	449	14
Unmarried, no partner	782	24
Number of children		
0	1753	55
1	594	19
2	669	21
3+	180	6
History of spontaneous abortion		
0	2782	87
1	299	9
2	61	2
3+	24	1
Do not know/do not want to answer	30	1
History of induced abortion		
0	2871	90
1	221	7
2	52	2
3+	22	1
Do not know/do not want to answer	30	1
Infertility consultation/treatment		
Never	2563	80
Ever (without ART[b])	365	11
Ever received ART	87	3

(continued)

Table 2.2 (continued)

Characteristics	*n*	Proportions (%)
Do not know/do not want to answer	181	6
Current contraceptive use		
None	638	20
Unreliable	1635	51
Reliable	923	29
Frequency of sexual intercourse		
1+ day per week	374	12
1–3 days per month	694	22
Less than once a month	919	29
Do not know/do not want to answer	1209	38

[a]Highest education completed by the respondent or in which the respondent is currently enrolled
[b]Assisted reproductive technology, which is defined in this book as in vitro fertilization and micro-insemination but excludes artificial insemination

research should examine the possible demographic impact of the combination of increasing age at childbearing, low frequency of sexual intercourse, and prolonged duration of breastfeeding. Considering that both primary infertility and secondary infertility are prevalent among Japanese women [9], it is important to assess the possible impact of breastfeeding behavior on fertility outcomes.

Available national data suggest that the proportion of breastfeeding mothers decreased from 1985 to 2005 and then increased in 2015. According to the national nutrition survey on preschool children in Japan, the proportion of mothers who exclusively breast-feed at 1 month after delivery slightly decreased from 49.5% in 1985 to 42.4% in 2005 and then increased to 51.3% in 2015. At 3 months after delivery, the proportions were 39.6% in 1985, 38.0% in 2005, and 54.7% in 2015 [10]. Reflecting the increase of breastfeeding mothers, the proportion of mothers who exclusively bottle feed at 1 month after delivery decreased from 9.1% in 1985 to 3.6% in 2015. The proportion of mothers who exclusively bottle feed at 3 months after delivery also decreased, going from 28.5% in 1985 to 10.2% in 2015 [10]. To the best of our knowledge, the potential demographic impact (e.g., the effect on fertility or birth intervals) of such changes in breastfeeding patterns has not yet been examined in Japan.

Consistent with numerous previous studies conducted overseas [8], the limited data in Japan show that mothers with longer durations of breastfeeding have longer postpartum amenorrhea compared to mothers who breast-feed for shorter durations. In the 1981 Field Survey of Fertility, which targeted women in three communities (Suginami Ward in Tokyo, Fukuoka City, and Hirosaki City) in Japan, more than 50% of mothers with 6-month-old babies who exclusively breast-fed were still experiencing lactational amenorrhea, whereas the proportion was as low as 10% for mothers who exclusively formula fed [7, 11]. Although it is expected that the recent increase in the proportion of breastfeeding mothers in Japan has resulted in the prolonged duration of postpartum amenorrhea, we know of no recently published data on postpartum amenorrhea among Japanese women, with the exception of the indirect data from our own survey. Data from the biodemography project in 2014 indirectly reveal a prolonged duration of lactational amenorrhea among breastfeeding mothers. Among breastfeeding mothers (either exclusively or combined with formula milk), as many as 58% (with 0-year-old babies), 35% (with 1-year-old babies), and 14% (with 2-year-old babies) were experiencing postpartum amenorrhea at the time of survey, as indicated by an absence of menstrual bleeding in the past 6 months, whereas among nonbreastfeeding mothers, the corresponding proportions were only 10% (with 0-year-old babies), 11% (with 1-year-old babies), and 2% (with 2-year-old babies). Considering that the age at first marriage continues to increase in Japan [12] and that reproductive years during marriage are decreasing, the relative impact of postpartum amenorrhea on fertility may have increased. This hypothesis should be tested in future research.

These limited Japanese data on breastfeeding and postpartum amenorrhea show a clear contrast with reports from Western populations regarding duration [13]. According to a recent report published in the Lancet [14], the estimated proportion of mothers in Japan who breast-feed (either exclusively or not) their 12-month-old babies was 60%, compared with only 9% in Canada, 3% in Denmark, 9% in France, 23% in Germany, 19% in Italy, 23% in Spain, 0.5% in the UK, and 27% in the USA. These data suggest the possibility that the duration of postpartum amenorrhea might be longer for Japanese mothers compared to mothers in Western countries in general, indicating that the demographic impact of nursing on fertility may be more evident in Japanese populations than in Western settings.

2.3 Fecund Waiting Time to Conception

In this section, we will focus on TTP as measured by number of months or menstrual cycles between starting unprotected intercourse and conception. Strictly speaking, fecund waiting time to conception differs from TTP measured in general epidemiological surveys because a certain proportion of fetal loss is not observed due to limitations in detection. In addition, certain previous studies did not include couples who had not yet conceived, i.e., right-censored TTP, whereas other studies did. Even with these limitations, we believe it is useful to summarize available data on TTP and the cumulative probability of pregnancy among Japanese couples with references to certain previous studies conducted overseas. Because TTP in a population commonly shows skewed distribution with some very long TTP and certain studies include right-censored TTP, the cumulative probability of conception is easy to understand and commonly used in many previous studies. Additionally, using data from the biodemography project, we present descriptive statistics of right-censored TTP, i.e., the duration of unprotected intercourse that has not resulted in pregnancy. Right-censored TTP is not comparable to TTP but provides an idea of the number of nulliparous couples who are waiting more than 12 months to conceive, which is a commonly used cutoff for infertility.

Table 2.3 Probability of conception by duration of marriage among Japanese women [15]

Duration of marriage (years)	Probability of conception in each year (%)	Proportion of women not yet pregnant at the end of each year (%)	Probability of conception in later years among those who did not conceive by the end of each year (%)
1	67.9	32.1	68.8
2	40.5	19.1	47.5
3	18.7	15.5	35.4
4	12.9	13.5	25.8
5	8.8	12.4	18.7
7	3.5	11.4	12.1
10	0.7	10.9	7.7
15	0.4	10.3	1.8

Information regarding the basic characteristics of participants, survey year, and location is unknown.

In 1939, Shinoda [15] targeted 7500 married women (Table 2.3) and reported that 67.9% of the women became pregnant within 1 year after marriage. Among the women who did not conceive within 1 year after marriage, 68.8% became pregnant thereafter and the other 31.2% did not conceive by the time of the survey. More recently, Arakawa and colleagues [16, 17] conducted a series of studies in three areas in Japan to examine the possible effects of environmental exposure on TTP, targeting mothers who had never received infertility treatment. At a hospital in Tokyo, they distributed questionnaires to n = 132 pregnant women [with a mean age of 30.1 (4.6) years]. The range of TTP was 0–54 months, and the mean (SD) was 5.9 (9.2) months. In a study that examined the association between hair mercury concentration and TTP, the authors targeted 298 mothers aged 31.4 (4.2) years who delivered at two hospitals in a coastal area of the Tohoku district. The questionnaire was distributed to mothers at 3 days postpartum and collected the following day. A total of 180 women (60%) reported TTP ranging between 0 and 80 months with a mean of 5.1 (7.3) months. Another study of theirs examined the association between dioxin concentrations in breast milk and TTP, targeting 153 pregnant women [with a mean age of 28.6 (4.5) years] at two clinics in the Miyazaki prefecture. A total of 99 women (65%) reported TTP ranging from 0 to 53 months with a mean of 4.5 (7.5) months. All three of these studies included both nulliparous and parous women, and the mode of TTP was 1 month. In the series of studies by Arakawa and colleagues, the cumulative probability of pregnancy after 6 months of trying was approximately 80%, which is similar to data from previous studies overseas. A study targeting pregnant women in Denmark that examined the association between moderate alcohol consumption and TTP targeted $n = 39{,}612$ pregnant women, among whom $n = 29{,}844$ (75%) reported their pregnancy to be planned and provided TTP values [18]. Among these women, 48% reported TTP of 0–2 months, 21% reported TTP of 3–5 months, 16% reported 6–12 months, and 15% reported TTP longer than 12 months. Another study compared TTP between couples in European countries and Thai couples and reported that among primigravida women with planned pregnancies, 73.7% of the European women reported TTP equal to or shorter than 6 months and 74.8% of the Thai women reported the same TTP [19]. Among multigravida women, the corresponding proportions were 74.9% for European women and 66.8% for Thai women.

Although the proportion of women with TTP longer than 6 months did not substantially differ between Japanese and Western data when noncensored TTP was considered, much less is known about right-censored TTP, i.e., the duration of trying to conceive without success. According to Shinoda [15], less than 70% of newly married couples conceived within 12 months after marriage. Comparative data from more recent populations in Japan [20] show that this proportion varies greatly depending on the couples' ages and tends to be lower than that found in previous studies in Western settings. The proportion of women who conceived within 12 months after discontinuing contraception was 80% for those aged 24–26 years, 66% for those aged 30–32 years, and 48% for those aged 36–38 years [20].

To examine the distribution of right-censored TTP and its associated factors, we limit the biodemography project sample to nulliparous women who were not currently pregnant and were not using any contraceptives (n = 235).[1] We defined right-censored TTP[2] as the duration of unprotected intercourse without pregnancy that leads to a live birth. Right-censored TTP could not be obtained from 118 women (50%).[3] Among those who reported valid right-censored TTP values (n = 117), 15% (n = 18) reported 0–11 months and 28% (n = 33) reported 10 years or longer (Fig. 2.1). As many as 85% of the couples reported right-censored TTP equal to or longer than 12 months. These data suggest that the nulliparous group comprised both women who had recently discontinued contraception and women who had been waiting to conceive for years. The median (interquartile range) of right-censored TTP for the 118 women was 63 (25, 130) months.

In addition, we explored several factors that potentially affect right-censored TTP in this limited sample of the biodemography project. We found that couples who received ART reported longer right-censored TTP compared to other women. For those who had never undergone infertility treatment, the right-censored TTP was 54 (19, 119) months, whereas for those who had undergone general infertility treatment, it was 56 (21, 124) months, and for those who had ever received ART, it was 84 (54, 124) months. Women with lower coital frequency reported longer

[1]Total number of participants in the biodemography project was n = 3196, among whom n = 1965 (61%) were married. Among the married women, n = 562 were nulliparous and currently not pregnant; among this smaller group, n = 235 were not using any contraception.

[2]For n = 89 women who reported that they had never used contraceptives, the right-censored TTP was defined as the duration between marriage and the time of the survey. For n = 146 women who reported that they had stopped using contraceptives, the right-censored TTP was defined as the duration between the cessation of contraceptive use and the time of survey.

[3]n = 23 did not report the month and year of marriage, and n = 95 did not report the month and year they discontinued contraception.

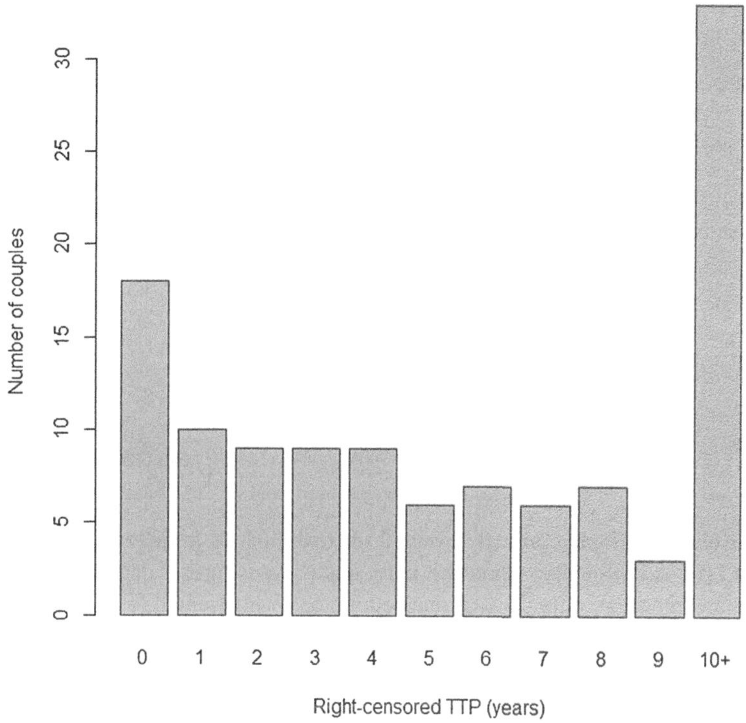

Fig. 2.1 Distribution of right-censored TTP for 118 married nulliparous women who were not pregnant at the time of the survey and were not using contraception. Data obtained from the 2014 biodemography project [1]

right-censored TTP. The median (interquartile range) was 25 (10, 41) months for women with 1 day or more of intercourse per week, 33 (7, 52) months for women with 1–3 days of intercourse per week, 98 (61, 152) months for those having intercourse less than once a month, and 84 (43, 160) months for those who did not report coital frequency. These data suggest that low coital frequency is common among couples who had not been using contraceptives for years but had not yet conceived.

2.4 Frequency of Sexual Intercourse

Frequency of sexual intercourse is one of the most influential components of fecund waiting time to conception. Recent research suggests that frequency of sexual intercourse tends to be lower among Japanese couples compared to couples overseas (e.g., [1,21]).

Table 2.4 Frequency of sexual intercourse during the past 6 months among married women in Japan by age at the time of the survey (unweighted %, n = 1965)

Frequency	Wife's age at the time of the survey (years)					
	20–24	25–29	30–34	35–39	40–44	Total
1+ day per week	11 (31%)	56 (22%)	72 (16%)	55 (9%)	57 (9%)	251 (13%)
1–3 days per month	14 (39%)	100 (39%)	149 (32%)	167 (28%)	111 (18%)	541 (28%)
Less than once a month	8 (22%)	70 (27%)	169 (37%)	271 (46%)	314 (51%)	832 (42%)
Do not know/do not want to answer	3 (8%)	32 (12%)	71 (15%)	101 (17%)	134 (22%)	341 (17%)
Total	36 (100%)	258 (100%)	461 (100%)	594 (100%)	616 (100%)	1965 (100%)

Number and proportions in each age category. Data obtained from the 2014 biodemography project [1]

The biodemography project revealed an overall low frequency of intercourse (Table 2.4). Additionally, when the participants were further categorized by their pregnancy intention, only 24% of married women who wanted to become pregnant and were not pregnant at the time of the survey were having intercourse 1+ day per week [1]. The proportion of women having intercourse 1+ day per week was even smaller for those who wanted to become pregnant in the future (14%) or who did not want to become pregnant (12%) [1]. The National Survey of Work and Family in Japan conducted in 2007 [21] also reported low coital frequency (Table 2.5); only 23% of women desiring a child had sexual intercourse at least once a week. The same survey showed that 21% of women aged between 20 and 29 years and 37% of women aged between 30 and 39 years were in sexless marriages, which refers to married or cohabitating couples who have not had any sexual intercourse for more than 1 month (Table 2.5, sum of "once in 2 months", "once in 6 months", and "not at all") [21]. In a series of studies conducted by Arakawa and colleagues [16] to examine a possible association between chemical exposure and TTP, more than 70% of the respondents answered that the frequency of intercourse before their latest pregnancy was equal to or less than once a week (Table 2.6). These data suggest that the frequency of intercourse tends to be low among couples in Japan today, even when the sample is limited to couples who eventually achieved pregnancy or were actively trying to conceive.

Although they are not directly comparable, previous studies conducted in Western settings seem to report higher frequencies of intercourse compared to previous studies conducted in Japan. A study based on the 2002 National Study of Family Growth of the USA revealed that the mean coital frequency for married women aged 25–45 years was 6.59 (95% CI: 6.27–6.91) times per month [22]. A study targeting pregnant women in the UK reported that the mean coital frequency before pregnancy was 1.9 (95% CI: 1.8, 1.9) times per week for fecund

Table 2.5 Frequency of marital intercourse during the past year (weighted %) by wife's age

Frequency of sexual intercourse	Age of women (years)				Total (n = 2464) (%)
	20–29 (n = 143) (%)	30–39 (n = 683) (%)	40–49 (n = 756) (%)	50–59 (n = 844) (%)	
1+ per week	29	19	12	8	14
Once every 2 weeks	25	14	12	10	13
Once a month	15	17	13	11	13
Once every 2 months	4	6	8	5	6
Once every 6 months	10	16	15	15	15
Never	7	15	24	37	24
Other	2	2	1	0	1
No answer	8	11	15	14	13
Total	100	100	100	100	100

Data obtained from the National Survey of Work and Family in Japan, 2007 [21]

Table 2.6 Mean (SD) age of mothers at the time of the survey and distribution (n and % in each study area) of the frequency of sexual intercourse before the current pregnancy

	Tokyo (n = 68)	Tohoku (coast) (n = 149)	Tohoku (city) (n = 297)	Miyazaki (n = 153)
Age (years)	30.1 (4.6)	29.2 (5.1)	31.4 (4.2)	28.6 (4.5)
Frequency of sexual intercourse (n)				
2+ times a week	16 (24%)	42 (28%)	51 (17%)	32 (21%)
Once a week	15 (22%)	59 (40%)	99 (33%)	76 (50%)
Less than once a week	36 (53%)	48 (32%)	120 (40%)	44 (29%)
Unknown	1 (1%)	0 (0%)	27 (9%)	1 (1%)

Questions were posed to pregnant women (mothers) in four places in Japan between 2000 and 2005 [16]

women (TTP $\leq$ 12 months) and 1.9 (95% CI: 1.8, 2.0) for subfecund women (TTP > 12 months) [23]. In a prospective cohort study on TTP targeting 2820 Danish women trying to conceive, the proportion of participants reporting 4 or more times of intercourse per week was 30.7% for women aged <25 years, 20.7% for women aged 25–29 years, 14.8% for women aged 30–34 years, and 15.4% for women aged 35–40 years at the baseline [24].

Although recent studies report relatively low frequency of sexual intercourse among Japanese couples compared to those in Western countries, studies conducted in the past report a higher frequency of intercourse among Japanese couples. For example, in 1955, Tsukamoto [25] reported that more than 80% of married women had sexual intercourse once a week or more (Table 2.7). Infrequent sexual

Table 2.7 Frequency of sexual intercourse among married women in agricultural villages in Yamanashi and Saitama prefectures in Japan (n = 97) [25]

Frequency of sexual intercourse	Right after marriage (n = 97)	At the time of the survey by women's age (years) and total				
		20–29 (n = 23)	30–39 (n = 34)	40–49 (n = 23)	50–59 (n = 7)	Total (n = 88)
8+ times a week	5 (5%)	0 (0%)	0 (0%)	0 (0%)	0 (0%)	0 (0%)
4–7 times a week	57 (59%)	4 (17%)	3 (9%)	1 (4%)	0 (0%)	8 (9%)
1–3 times a week	35 (36%)	19 (83%)	29 (82%)	14 (61%)	2 (29%)	65 (74%)
Less than once a week	0 (0%)	0 (0%)	2 (6%)	4 (17%)	4 (57%)	10 (11%)
Almost never	0 (0%)	0 (0%)	0 (0%)	4 (17%)	1 (14%)	5 (6%)
Total						

Frequency of intercourse is shown separately for immediately after marriage and at the time of survey (by women's age and total). The survey was conducted between 1953 and 1954

intercourse among Japanese couples in recent years may be the result of socio-cultural factors, including prevalent premarital sex [26], higher unemployment rates, and long working hours among those who are employed [27]. It is also possible that a lower frequency of marital sexual intercourse is often accompanied by active sexual activity outside the marital relationship, although we do not have sufficient data to support or reject this supposition.

2.5 Menstrual Cycle

Menstrual cycle abnormalities, such as irregularity and short or long cycle lengths, have been linked to infertility, particularly through ovulation disorders and longer TTP [28–31]. The Japan Society of Obstetrics and Gynecology defines a normal menstrual cycle length as between 25 and 38 days and defines a regular cycle as that with a length that changes by less than 7 days [32]. A seminal study by Matsumoto [33] on 701 housewives of coal miners found that their average cycle length was 30.37 days (SD = 6.54 days) and that the average shift[4] in menstrual cycle length was 8.15 days (SD = 5.98 days).

Using data from the biodemography project, we present our analysis on cycle length and regularity of menstruation.[5] Short and long menstrual cycles are often related to anovulation, which prolongs TTP [28, 31]. According to

[4]Cycle length variation was calculated by taking the difference between the maximum and minimum lengths among 10 consecutive ovulatory cycles randomly selected from 65 subjects.

[5]Appendix shows the original survey questionnaire items used to measure cycle length and regularity.

Table 2.8 Cross-tab between cycle lengths and cycle irregularity[a] (n = 2454)

		Regular Cycle	Irregular Cycle	Total
Short cycle (<25 days)	N	51	32	83
	%	61	39	100
Normal cycle (25–37 days)	N	1170	747	1917
	%	61	39	100
Long cycle (>37 days)	N	7	43	50
	%	14	86	100
No particular cycle length	N	59	345	404
	%	15	85	100
Total	n	1287	1167	2454
	%	52	48	100

Data obtained from the 2014 biodemography project [1]
[a]Cycle irregularity is defined as changes in cycle length of 7+ days during the past 6 months

Matsumoto [33], anovulation, as measured by basal body temperature, was much more prevalent (approximately 17%) among short (<25 days) and long (>38 days) cycles than among normal cycles, where only 3.2% were anovulatory. Cycle length variability commonly occurs a few years after menarche and before menopause and has been found to be related to lower fecundability [34, 35] and a history of fetal loss and infertility[6] [36]. In analyzing our data, we selected women who were not pregnant or breastfeeding and who had experienced menstruation at least once in the past 6 months. We excluded women who took steroids or other hormonal medicine in the 3 months prior to the survey. The sample size for the current selection is 2454.

Our data show that among respondents who reported their cycle lengths (n = 2050), the average menstrual cycle length was 28.9 days with a standard deviation of 3.7 days. Approximately 94% of the reported cycle lengths fell within the normal length of 25–38 days. Regarding cycle irregularity, 37% of respondents have experienced an irregular menstrual cycle with more than 6 days of shift. Additionally, approximately 10% of respondents reported that their cycle is too irregular to know whether they have experienced a cycle length shift. Table 2.8 shows the cross-tabulation between cycle lengths and cycle irregularity. Approximately 86% of women with long cycle lengths reported that they have experienced cycle irregularity of more than 6 days, whereas approximately 60% of those with short or normal cycle lengths indicated that they have never experienced cycle irregularity. Among those who indicated that they do not have a fixed cycle length, approximately 15% of them stated that they have a regular cycle, i.e., they have not experienced a change in cycle length greater than 6 days even though they do not have a fixed schedule.

[6]Infertility is defined as more than one year of having unprotected intercourse without pregnancy.

To better understand how social and behavioral factors affect the length and irregularity of menstrual cycles, we conducted multivariate analyses. For the analysis of menstrual cycle length, we used the following three categories for the dependent variable: short (<25 days) cycle, long (>38 days) cycle, and normal (25–38 days) cycle. Approximately 3% of the sample reported having short cycles ($n = 83$), and approximately 2% reported having long cycles ($n = 50$). We used a multinomial logistic regression with normal cycle length as a reference group. For the analysis of irregularity, we defined irregularity as a change in cycle length by more than 6 days in the past 6 months; we also included those whose cycles are too irregular to report. Overall, those who reported irregularity constitute 48% ($n = 1167$) of the total sample. Our independent variables are age, parity, educational background, BMI, smoking, and work hours per week.

Table 2.9 indicates that compared to 30–34-year-old women, women who are younger than 30 years are more likely to have irregular menstrual cycles, whereas

Table 2.9 Effect of lifestyle factors on menstrual cycle irregularity. Odds ratios and 95% confidence intervals from binomial logistic regressions ($n = 2454$)

Explanatory variables	Irregular menstrual cycle
Age (years)	
20–24	2.18 (1.57, 3.03)
25–29	1.31 (0.99, 1.74)
30–34	Reference
35–39	0.73 (0.57, 0.92)
40–44	0.81 (0.64, 1.02)
Parity	
Nulliparous	Reference
Parous	0.91 (0.61, 1.36)
Education	
HS or less	Reference
Vocational school	0.91 (0.75, 1.12)
College+	0.86 (0.70, 1.06)
BMI	
Underweight (<18.5)	1.31 (1.06, 1.62)
Normal (18.5–25)	Reference
Overweight (25+)	1.47 (1.13, 1.91)
Smoking	
No (never or former)	Reference
Current	1.17 (0.91, 1.49)
Work hours per week	
0 h	Reference
1–34 h	0.97 (0.79, 1.19)
35–49 h	1.03 (0.84, 1.26)
50+ h	1.49 (1.03, 2.14)

Data obtained from the 2014 biodemography project [1]

Table 2.10 Effect of lifestyle factors on menstrual cycle length

Explanatory variables	Short cycle (<25 days)	Long cycle (>38 days)
Age (years)		
20–24	3.05 (1.19, 7.81)	0.95 (0.36, 2.52)
25–29	1.63 (0.61, 4.30)	0.95 (0.42, 2.17)
30–34	Reference	Reference
35–39	2.08 (0.91, 4.73)	0.57 (0.26, 1.24)
40–44	2.50 (1.13, 5.53)	0.29 (0.12, 0.72)
Parity		
Nulliparous	Reference	Reference
Parous	3.84 (0.52, 28.17)	1.20 (0.28, 5.14)
Education		
HS or less	Reference	Reference
Vocational school	0.79 (0.45, 1.37)	0.95 (0.45, 2.01)
College+	0.89 (0.51, 1.35)	1.25 (0.61, 2.55)
BMI		
Underweight (<18.5)	1.09 (0.61, 1.95)	1.21 (0.60, 2.45)
Normal (18.5–25)	Reference	Reference
Overweight (25+)	1.05 (0.51, 2.16)	1.94 (0.87, 4.33)
Smoking		
No (never or former)	Reference	Reference
Current	1.89 (1.06, 3.35)	1.80 (0.84, 3.86)
Work hours per week		
0 h	Reference	Reference
1–34 h	2.45 (1.36, 4.41)	1.05 (0.52, 2.12)
35–49 h	1.26 (0.66, 2.40)	0.69 (0.33, 1.44)
50+ h	1.65 (0.59, 4.62)	0.83 (0.23, 2.96)

Odds ratios and 95% confidence intervals from multinomial logistic regressions (Ref = 25–37 days, n = 2050). Data obtained from the 2014 biodemography project [1]

those older than 35 years are less likely to report cycle irregularity. Underweight and overweight women are more likely to have irregular menstrual cycles. Data also show that women who work 50+ hours per week are approximately 50% more likely to experience irregular menstrual cycles compared with women who do not work at all. With respect to short (<25 days) menstrual cycles (Table 2.10), as compared to the normal cycle length of 25–38 days, 25–34-year-old women are less likely to have short cycles than women in all other age-groups. Smoking appears to increase the risk of short menstrual cycles by 89%. In addition, women who work part-time (1–34 h per week) are at a greater risk of having a short menstrual cycle than women who do not work at all. Regarding long (>38 days) cycles, we did not find any strong associations except that 40–44-year-old women are much less likely to report long cycles compared to 30–34-year-old respondents. The effect of age on cycle lengths is somewhat in line with previous studies, which report shorter cycle lengths after age 35 years and several years prior to menopause [37, 38].

Our analyses suggest that social and behavioral factors have different effects on menstrual cycle irregularity and length. For example, BMI has a consistent effect on irregular menstruation, whereas smoking increases the risk of a short menstrual cycle. Work hours are also important, given that an increasing number of women continue to work after marriage [39]. Our data also suggest that overwork (i.e., 50+ hours per week) may increase irregular menstrual cycles, whereas part-time work (i.e., 1–34 h per week) may be linked to short menstrual cycles. Future studies may investigate the effect of women's work and family environments on menstrual cycle characteristics.

2.6 Use of Contraception

Contraception affects fecund waiting time to conception either by decreasing the frequency of insemination (e.g., barrier methods) or by decreasing the proportion of ovulatory cycles (e.g., oral contraceptives). As reported in many previous studies (e.g., [1, 16, 18]), the use of oral contraceptive pills is not yet very common in Japan, where the male condom remains the most frequently used contraceptive method. According to the Japan National Fertility Survey (JNFS) conducted in 2005, the proportion of never-married sexually active women aged 18–34 years who used contraceptive pills at their most recent sexual intercourse was only 1.6%, whereas 73.9% used condoms and 9.4% used withdrawal [26]. Another survey, which targeted a nationally representative sample of women aged between 16 and 49 years and was conducted in 2002, revealed that only 3.5% of respondents currently used oral contraceptives [40]. More recently, using biodemography study data, Konishi and Tamaki [1] reported that 2% of married women and 10% of unmarried (and partnered) women always used contraceptive pills, whereas the proportions using condoms were 30% for married women and 48% for unmarried (and partnered) women (Tables 2.11 and 2.12).

Cultural, historical, and/or sociological backgrounds of the current contraceptive behavior of Japanese couples is beyond the focus of this book, but the low prevalence of contraceptive pill use among Japanese women may be a reflection of the recent approval of low-dose contraceptive pills (in 1999), low coital frequency, and/or a high artificial abortion rate. Unreliable contraceptive use and the associated risks of unintended pregnancy among nonmarried couples are expected to play an important role in fertility trends in this country. One fact that supports this notion is that an increasing proportion of couples marry following premarital pregnancy [41]. Therefore, fertility intention, together with detailed data on contraceptive behavior and the probability of conception, should be thoroughly investigated in future research to understand the mechanism of fertility trends in this setting.

Table 2.11 Current contraceptive use by married women in Japan (n = 1361)[a]

Type of contraceptive	Always use	Sometimes use	Stopped using	Never used	Do not know/ do not want to answer
Condom	409 (30%)	277 (20%)	500 (37%)	175 (13%)	0 (0%)
Oral contraceptive	24 (2%)	5 (0%)	117 (9%)	1215 (89%)	0 (0%)
Emergency pill	0 (0%)	0 (0%)	22 (2%)	1333 (98%)	6 (0%)
Withdrawal	140 (10%)	195 (14%)	204 (15%)	682 (50%)	140 (10%)
Calendar	131 (10%)	149 (11%)	215 (16%)	826 (61%)	40 (3%)
Basal body temperature	119 (9%)	76 (6%)	460 (34%)	689 (51%)	17 (1%)
Other	25 (2%)	24 (2%)	31 (2%)	919 (68%)	362 (27%)

Data obtained from the 2014 biodemography project [1]
[a]Sample is limited to women who were not pregnant at the time of the survey, had menstruated in the past 6 months, answered the question regarding the frequency of condom and oral contraceptive use, and neither were sterilized nor had a partner who was sterilized. See [1] for the definition of the analytic sample

Table 2.12 Current contraceptive use of unmarried women with a partner (n = 385)[a] in Japan

	Always use	Sometimes use	Stopped using	Never used	Do not know/do not want to answer	Total
Condom	184 (48%)	84 (22%)	79 (21%)	38 (10%)	0 (0%)	385 (100%)
Oral contraceptive	38 (10%)	4 (1%)	40 (10%)	303 (79%)	0 (0%)	385 (100%)
Emergency pill (morning pill)	0 (0%)	2 (1%)	20 (5%)	358 (93%)	5 (1%)	385 (100%)
Withdrawal	47 (12%)	69 (18%)	41 (11%)	204 (53%)	24 (6%)	385 (100%)
Calendar	52 (14%)	48 (12%)	19 (5%)	260 (68%)	6 (2%)	385 (100%)
Basal body temperature	30 (8%)	23 (6%)	64 (17%)	263 (68%)	5 (1%)	385 (100%)
Other	3 (1%)	2 (1%)	5 (1%)	263 (68%)	112 (29%)	385 (100%)

Data obtained from the 2014 biodemography project [1]
[a]Sample is limited to women who were not pregnant at the time of the survey, had menstruated in the past 6 months, answered the question regarding the frequency of condom and oral contraceptive use, and neither were sterilized nor had a partner who was sterilized. See [1] for the definition of the analytic sample

2.7 Infertility Treatment

Infertility treatment may affect fecund waiting time to conception in various ways. Assisted reproductive technology (ART) can possibly shorten time to conception for couples who have obvious reproductive issues and could never conceive naturally. However, the extent to which TTP may be shortened for couples without any obvious reasons for infertility is unknown. For example, a 2016 Cochrane review article reported that for couples with unexplained infertility, there is no firm evidence of an increased cumulative live birth rate among couples undergoing artificial insemination versus those trying to conceive with timed intercourse [42]. According to a 2015 Cochrane review article, in vitro fertilization may yield a higher cumulative live birthrate compared with expectant management or artificial insemination, but there is insufficient evidence to draw a firm conclusion [43]. Considering that Japan had the world's highest number of infertility treatment cycles in 2010 [44], interrelationships between ART and TTP and between ART and the cumulative pregnancy rate should be thoroughly studied in future research.

According to the world report of the International Committee for Monitoring Assisted Reproductive Technologies, Japan recorded 153,729 aspirations for fresh in vitro fertilization and micro-insemination and 242,833 frozen embryo transfer cycles in 2010 [44]. These numbers were much higher than those in the USA (81,075 aspirations and 176,214 frozen embryo transfer cycles), which ranked second in terms of the number of aspirations in the same year. In Japan, pregnancy rate per aspiration was 9.3% and delivery rate per aspiration was 6.2% in 2010 (considering only fresh cycles), which are lower than the means, i.e., 27.0 and 20.1%, respectively, for all countries (approximately $n = 60$) listed in the report. When both fresh and frozen embryo transfer cycles were considered, the estimated cumulative delivery rate per aspiration was 18.1% for Japan, which again is lower than the figure (27.1%) for all listed countries. The relatively low rate of success may partly be related to the fact that compared with many other countries, Japan is characterized by a smaller number of embryos transferred to the mother's uterus at one time. In fact, 70.0% of the 65,024 fresh nondonor IVF and ICSI cycles constituted single embryo transfers, whereas only 28.5% involved transfers of 2 embryos and 1.6% involved transfers of 3+ embryos, which is probably linked to low multiple birthrates (5.3% twin births and 0.1% triplet+ births) in 2010. Among all countries listed in the paper, the corresponding proportions were 20.4% for twin births and 1.1% for triplet+ births [44].

The high number of ART cycles conducted in Japan may reflect three possible factors, none of which are necessarily exclusive: (1) Compared to other populations, more Japanese couples may be experiencing infertility, i.e., longer TTP; (2) Japanese couples are more likely to consult a doctor about infertility issues; and (3) once couples in Japan begin infertility treatment, they are more likely to undergo ART. With the currently available data, we cannot determine which factors are more or less important and thus it is worth examining what factors contribute to the very frequent use of ART in Japan.

Using data obtained from the biodemography project, we report preliminary results regarding who is more likely to have undergone infertility treatment (ART or any other kind) (Tables 2.13 and 2.14). Here, a woman is considered to have undergone ART if she has ever undergone either in vitro fertilization and/or micro-insemination. If a woman ever visited a doctor for treatment of and/or consultation for infertility, she was deemed to have received infertility treatment. The "any other infertility treatment" category in Table 2.13 includes those who have ever undergone a medical examination for infertility and/or utilized the timing method, ovulation induction, and/or artificial insemination but excludes women who have ever undergone ART. In this study population, we find that ART is common across all socioeconomic status subgroups (Table 2.13), but our multivariate analysis revealed that women with household incomes less than 3 million yen were less likely to have received infertility treatment (Table 2.14). In Table 2.14, the "any infertility treatment" category includes those who received ART. Compared to nulliparous women, parous and especially multiparous women are significantly less likely to have experienced either type (ART or other) of infertility treatment. This result may reflect the fact that many women who have undergone infertility treatments have not yet succeeded in having children. Infrequent sexual intercourse was significantly associated with higher odds of having undergone infertility treatment. Due to the cross-sectional study design, we cannot tell whether couples had infrequent sex as a result of infertility treatments or if couples who had infrequent sexual intercourse were more likely to undergo such treatments. Although we should await further research to test whether the causal link exists, it can be noted that infertility treatment seems to be closely linked to frequency of sexual intercourse, which is one of the most influential proximate determinants of fertility.

Here, we summarize findings related to infertility treatment based on previous studies that targeted nationally representative populations. Using data from the 13th National Fertility Survey in 2005, Iwasawa and Mita [9] estimate that proportion of married women at reproductive ages who ever had infertility treatment was 13% and that the proportion who were currently receiving infertility treatment was 1.2%. They also argue that the number of couples receiving infertility treatment not only reflects the number of infertile couples but also behavioral differences, i.e., the tendency to consult with medical doctors. The 14th National Fertility Survey in 2010 showed that 31.1% of married couples (with wives ranging in age from 20 to 29 years) reported that they "had ever worried about infertility" [45]. The proportion of married couples (with wives ranging in age between 20 and 49 years) who had ever had clinical tests or treatments for fertility was 16.4%. The proportions were even higher when the sample was limited to nulliparous couples; 28.6% actually had infertility tests or treatment [45]. These data suggest that an increasing proportion of couples are unable to have children and that more couples are worried about their own fecundity today than in the past in part because of increased awareness of fertility issues.

The prevalence of ART among couples in Japan is evidenced by the fact that 3.7% of all live births resulted from conceptions achieved through ART [46].

Table 2.13 Basic characteristics of married women by experience with infertility treatment (n = 1852)

Explanatory variables	ART[a] (n = 85)	Any other infertility treatment[b] (n = 329)	No infertility treatment (n = 1438)	Total (n = 1852)
Parity				
Nulliparous	43 (51%)	120 (36%)	406 (28%)	569 (31%)
Primiparous	24 (28%)	98 (30%)	393 (27%)	515 (28%)
Multiparous	18 (21%)	111 (34%)	639 (44%)	768 (41%)
Wife's age at the time of the survey (years)				
20–24	0 (0%)	2 (1%)	34 (2%)	36 (2%)
25–29	3 (4%)	24 (7%)	219 (15%)	246 (13%)
30–34	17 (20%)	100 (30%)	316 (22%)	433 (23%)
35–39	34 (40%)	115 (35%)	412 (29%)	561 (30%)
40–44	31 (36%)	88 (27%)	457 (32%)	576 (31%)
Wife's age at the time of marriage (years)				
<20	2 (2%)	4 (1%)	23 (2%)	29 (2%)
20–24	4 (5%)	66 (20%)	351 (24%)	421 (23%)
25–29	42 (49%)	162 (49%)	615 (43%)	819 (44%)
30–34	23 (27%)	75 (23%)	289 (20%)	387 (21%)
35–39	8 (9%)	17 (5%)	82 (6%)	107 (6%)
40+	2 (2%)	1 (0%)	13 (1%)	16 (1%)
Duration of marriage (years)				
0–4	22 (26%)	95 (29%)	486 (34%)	603 (33%)
5–9	29 (34%)	124 (38%)	366 (25%)	519 (28%)
10–14	24 (28%)	73 (22%)	319 (22%)	416 (22%)
15+	6 (7%)	33 (10%)	198 (14%)	237 (13%)

(continued)

Table 2.13 (continued)

Explanatory variables	ART[a] (*n* = 85)	Any other infertility treatment[b] (*n* = 329)	No infertility treatment (*n* = 1438)	Total (*n* = 1852)
Highest educational level[c]				
Less than college	20 (24%)	80 (24%)	448 (31%)	548 (30%)
College	33 (39%)	133 (40%)	536 (37%)	702 (38%)
University	32 (38%)	116 (35%)	454 (32%)	602 (33%)
Annual household income (million yen)				
<3	12 (14%)	53 (16%)	332 (23%)	397 (21%)
3–4	24 (28%)	121 (37%)	457 (32%)	602 (33%)
5–9	30 (35%)	125 (38%)	445 (31%)	600 (32%)
10+	19 (22%)	30 (9%)	204 (14%)	253 (14%)
Intention of becoming pregnant				
Currently want (within 1 year from now)	51 (60%)	153 (47%)	309 (21%)	513 (28%)
Want in the future (more than 1 year from now)	2 (2%)	26 (8%)	172 (12%)	200 (11%)
No	32 (38%)	150 (46%)	957 (67%)	1139 (62%)
Smoking				
No (never or former)	79 (93%)	303 (92%)	1272 (88%)	1654 (89%)
Current	6 (7%)	26 (8%)	166 (12%)	198 (11%)
Menstrual cycle characteristics[d]				
Regular	36 (42%)	114 (35%)	576 (40%)	726 (39%)
Short	12 (14%)	38 (12%)	178 (12%)	228 (12%)
Long	24 (28%)	101 (31%)	453 (32%)	578 (31%)
Irregular	13 (15%)	76 (23%)	228 (16%)	317 (17%)
Never	0 (0%)	0 (0%)	3 (0%)	3 (0%)

(continued)

Table 2.13 (continued)

Explanatory variables	ART[a] (*n* = 85)	Any other infertility treatment[b] (*n* = 329)	No infertility treatment (*n* = 1438)	Total (*n* = 1852)
Frequency of sexual intercourse[e]				
1+ day per week	7 (8%)	45 (14%)	197 (14%)	249 (13%)
1–3 days per month	19 (22%)	100 (30%)	418 (29%)	537 (29%)
<1 day per month	42 (49%)	155 (47%)	619 (43%)	816 (44%)
Unknown	17 (20%)	29 (9%)	204 (14%)	250 (13%)

A total of 113 married women who did not answer the question regarding infertility treatment were excluded. Numbers and proportions in each category (i.e., ART, any other infertility treatment, no infertility treatment, and total) are shown. Data obtained from the 2014 biodemography project [1]

[a]Ever used assisted reproductive technology, i.e., in vitro fertilization or micro-insemination

[b]Ever visited a doctor for treatment of and/or consultation for infertility. This category includes those who have ever undergone a medical examination for infertility and/or employed the timing method, ovulation induction, and/or artificial insemination but excludes women who have ever used ART

[c]Highest education level completed or in which respondent is currently enrolled

[d]Participating women were asked either to state their ordinal menstrual cycle length or to choose one of the following answers: "cycle length is irregular (and there is no ordinal cycle length)" or "have never experienced menstrual bleeding." If stated cycle length was shorter than 27 days, the respondent was categorized as having a short cycle, and if stated cycle length was equal to or longer than 30 days, the respondent was categorized as having a long cycle. Respondents were categorized as having regular cycles if the reported cycle length was between 27 and 29 days

[e]In the past 6 months

Although it is true that couples who are unable to have a child without ART are now able to do so with the help of medical technology, the success rate of ART steadily declines as women age and thus ART can overcome age-related decline in fecundity only to a certain extent. Data on the success rates of ART accumulated by the Japan Society of Obstetrics and Gynecology clearly show that age-related decline of fecundability is evident among pregnancies resulting from ART. In 2012, live birthrates per ART cycle were 21.8% for 30-year-old women, 17.3% for 35-year-old women, 8.1% for 40-year-old women, and 0.7% for 45-year-old women [47]. These data clearly indicate that decreased fecundability due to aging cannot be fully overcome by ART. Related to this notion, Leridon uses a simulation model and suggests that ART in its present form is unable to address the loss of births due to age-related decreases in fecundability [48]. Although studies from overseas that included both censored and noncensored TTP report that age-related decline in fecundability starts at around age 30 years or in the mid-30s [24, 49, 50], Konishi et al. [20] report, based on TTP for the first child, that fecundability was highest among couples who discontinued contraception when the wife was aged 24–26 years and was significantly lower for older ages. Future research targeting

Table 2.14 Odds ratios (95% confidence interval) of having experienced ART or any infertility treatment by participant characteristics (n = 1852 married women)

Explanatory variable	ART[a]	Any infertility treatment[b]
Parity		
Nulliparous	1.00	1.00
Primiparous	0.70 (0.40, 1.22)	0.74 (0.54, 1.00)
Multiparous	0.52 (0.26, 1.03)	0.70 (0.50, 0.97)
Wife's age at marriage (years)		
25–29	1.00	1.00
<20	1.97 (0.39, 10.12)	1.08 (0.40, 2.90)
20–24	0.21 (0.07, 0.62)	0.70 (0.50, 0.99)
30–34	1.22 (0.69, 2.18)	0.96 (0.70, 1.31)
35–39	2.50 (1.01, 6.17)	1.25 (0.73, 2.13)
40+	9.17 (1.68, 50.16)	1.65 (0.41, 6.58)
Duration of marriage (years)		
0–4	1.00	1.00
5–9	2.98 (1.57, 5.68)	3.32 (2.37, 4.65)
10–14	6.22 (2.82, 13.72)	3.75 (2.47, 5.69)
15+	4.73 (1.49, 15.02)	3.06 (1.79, 5.24)
Highest educational level[c]		
Less than college	1.00	1.00
College	0.83 (0.44, 1.57)	1.19 (0.87, 1.63)
University	0.91 (0.47, 1.75)	1.20 (0.86, 1.68)
Annual household income (million yen)		
3–4	1.00	1.00
<3	0.74 (0.34, 1.60)	0.60 (0.42, 0.86)
5–9	1.25 (0.69, 2.27)	1.05 (0.79, 1.41)
10+	1.58 (0.78, 3.19)	0.71 (0.47, 1.06)
Intention of becoming pregnant		
Currently want (within 1 year from now)	1.00	1.00
Want in the future (more than 1 year from now)	0.11 (0.03, 0.48)	0.26 (0.16, 0.41)
No	0.15 (0.08, 0.27)	0.17 (0.12, 0.23)
Smoking		
No (never or former)	1.00	1.00
Current	0.53 (0.20, 1.41)	0.73 (0.47, 1.13)

(continued)

Table 2.14 (continued)

Explanatory variable	ART[a]	Any infertility treatment[b]
Menstrual cycle characteristics[d]		
Regular	1.00	1.00
Short	1.05 (0.50, 2.21)	1.22 (0.82, 1.82)
Long	1.02 (0.57, 1.81)	1.18 (0.88, 1.58)
Irregular	1.14 (0.56, 2.33)	2.16 (1.54, 3.03)
Never	1.00	1.00
Frequency of sexual intercourse[e]		
1+ day per week	1.00	1.00
1–3 days per month	1.34 (0.53, 3.38)	1.16 (0.77, 1.73)
<1 day per month	2.28 (0.95, 5.47)	1.51 (1.02, 2.24)
Unknown	2.96 (1.11, 7.90)	1.09 (0.66, 1.80)

A total of 113 married women who did not answer the question regarding infertility treatment were excluded from the analysis. A logistic regression analysis was used, and all variables in the table were included as explanatory variables. Separate models were used for the ART experience (vs. no ART or no infertility treatment) and for any infertility treatment (vs. no infertility treatment). Data obtained from the 2014 biodemography project [1]

[a]Ever undergone in vitro fertilization or micro-insemination

[b]Ever visited a doctor for treatment of and/or consultation for infertility. This category includes women who have ever undergone a medical examination for infertility and/or utilized the timing method, ovulation induction, artificial insemination, and/or ART.

[c]Highest education level completed or in which respondent is currently enrolled

[d]Participants were asked either to report their ordinal menstrual cycle length or to select one of the following answers: "cycle length is irregular (there is no ordinal cycle length)" or "have never experienced menstrual bleeding." If the stated cycle length was shorter than 27 days, the respondent was categorized as having a short cycle, and if the stated cycle length was equal to or longer than 30 days, the respondent was categorized as having a long cycle. Respondents were categorized as having regular cycles if the reported cycle length was between 27 and 29 days

[e]In the past 6 months

the Japanese population is needed to assess the extent to which this age-related decline in fecundability can be compensated by efficient utilization of ART. The limited evidence available thus far clearly indicates that the use of ART is very common among couples, but the impact of infertility treatment on the fertility of a population has not yet been fully evaluated in this setting.

2.8 Fetal Loss

Fetal loss includes both spontaneous pregnancy loss (natural abortion) and induced (artificial) abortion. In this book, we define abortion as any pregnancy loss that occurs at any gestational age. The term "stillbirth" is not used in this book because there are several definitions of stillbirth and thus the terminology may be confusing.

For example, the World Health Organization defines stillbirths as "a baby born with no signs of life at or after 28 weeks' gestation" [51] whereas the Centers for Disease Control and Prevention of the USA maintains that "a stillbirth is the death of a baby before or during delivery" [52]. There is no universally accepted definition of when a fetal death is called a stillbirth, and the meaning of this term varies internationally.

2.8.1 Spontaneous Pregnancy Loss

When pregnancy tests with greater sensitivity are used, it is more likely that pregnancies that end during early gestational period will be detected. With less sensitive pregnancy tests, one is more likely to be unaware of those pregnancies and thus detect fewer pregnancy losses. Even with this limitation in detection, the age pattern of spontaneous pregnancy loss is clearly evident, as will be described below.

The probability of spontaneous pregnancy loss increases as a woman and man age. Figure 2.2 shows the ratios of the number of natural pregnancy losses to the number of live births in Japan and Denmark, both of which are based on national data ([53], see the footnote of Fig. 2.2 for data source). Although the ratios of the two countries differ with respect to certain age-groups, the age pattern of spontaneous pregnancy loss is similar between the two countries, with an evident increase

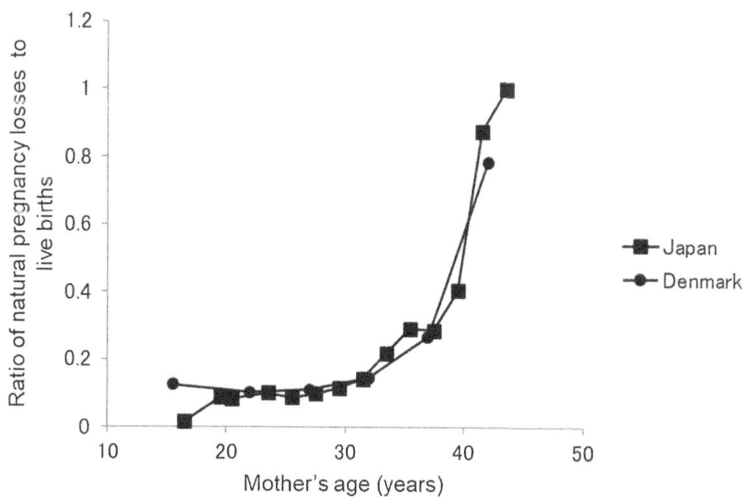

Fig. 2.2 Ratios of the number of natural pregnancy losses to the number of live births by mother's age at the time of pregnancy. Data obtained from [53]. The original data for Japan came from the 13th National Fertility Survey on married couples [58]. The sum of the numbers of first to fifth pregnancies was used to calculate the ratio of natural pregnancy losses to live births. The original data for Denmark came from [59]

Table 2.15 Proportions of married and single women in each age-group who had experienced spontaneous or induced abortion

Age (years)	Married			Single		
	n	Spontaneous	Induced	*n*	Spontaneous	Induced
20–24	36	19% (3%)	14% (0%)	243	0% (0%)	1% (0%)
25–29	258	11% (2%)	12% (2%)	263	1% (0%)	5% (1%)
30–34	461	16% (3%)	11% (3%)	246	2% (0%)	9% (3%)
35–39	594	18% (4%)	9% (2%)	222	6% (1%)	10% (4%)
40–44	616	21% (6%)	12% (3%)	211	6% (0%)	9% (2%)
Total	1965	18% (4%)	11% (2%)	1185	3% (0%)	7% (2%)

Percentages in parentheses indicate the proportions of women who had experienced two or more abortions in each category. Data obtained from the 2014 biodemography project [1]

when women reach their late 30s. These data indicate that as a woman ages, she faces a higher risk of pregnancy loss.

The biodemography project shows that more than 20% of married women aged 40–44 years had ever experienced spontaneous abortion (Table 2.15). This proportion is slightly higher than that in the National Fertility Survey of 2015 [54], in which the proportions of married couples who had ever experienced spontaneous abortions were 18.1% for couples married for 15–19 years and 17.6% for those married for more than 20 years.

2.8.2 *Artificial Abortion*

Although we have little evidence to believe that age patterns of spontaneous pregnancy loss vary significantly across populations, the rates of artificial abortion reflect sociocultural settings and vary across both populations and calendar years. In Japan, the induced abortion rate per 1000 women aged 15–49 years decreased from 14.9 in 1989 to 6.9 in 2014, which is lower than the induced abortion rate of developed countries (excluding eastern Europe), which was 17 in 2008 [55]. The low induced abortion rate in Japan seems to reflect a low number of total pregnancies rather than a lower proportion of pregnancies that end in induced abortions. According to Senda [53], in Japan in 2009, there were 1,070,029 live births and 223,388 induced abortions, yielding a ratio of induced abortions to live births of approximately 21% (223,388/1,070,029). In 1955, there were 1,730,689 live births and 1,169,079 induced abortions (1,169,079/1,730,689 = 68%). The corresponding proportions were 38% in 1970 and 37% in 1990. Reflecting the high proportion of pregnancies that end in induced abortion, it is estimated that among cohorts born in 1970, more than 20% of Japanese women experienced induced abortion by the age of 32.5 years [26].

According to the biodemography project, 9–14% of married women in each age-group experienced induced abortion (Table 2.15). Among single women aged

35–39 years, as many as 10% had experienced induced abortion. These data suggest that both married and single women conceive and experience fetal loss. Therefore, to understand the mechanisms of fertility trends, it is necessary to study the reproductive behavior of both married couples and single women and men.

Appendix: Survey Questionnaire Items in the Biodemography Project

1. How long is your menstrual cycle (not the length of menstrual bleeding but rather the length between the first day of one menstrual period and the first day of the next period)?

   1.1. About ( ) days
   1.2. No particular cycle length
   1.3. I have never experienced menstruation.

2. In the past 6 months, have you experienced any changes in the onset of a menstrual cycle by more than 6 days?

   2.1. Yes, I have experienced such a change at least once
   2.2. No, I have not experienced any change (almost always on schedule)
   2.3. My menstrual period is too irregular to know my usual schedule
   2.4. I have not menstruated in the past 6 months.

References

1. Konishi, Shoko, and Emi Tamaki. 2016. Pregnancy intention and contraceptive use among married and unmarried women in Japan. *Japanese Journal of Health and Human Ecology* 82: 110–124.
2. Slama, Rémy, Beatrice Ducot, Lisbeth Carstensen, Christine Lorente, Elise De La Rochebrochard, Henri Leridon, Niels Keiding, and Jean Bouyer. 2006. Feasibility of the current-duration approach to studying human fecundity. *Epidemiology* 17: 440–449.
3. Slama, R., O.K.H. Hansen, B. Ducot, A. Bohet, D. Sorensen, L. Giorgis Allemand, M.J.C. Eijkemans, et al. 2012. Estimation of the frequency of involuntary infertility on a nation-wide basis. *Human Reproduction* 27: 1489–1498.
4. Huybrechts, Krista F., Ellen M. Mikkelsen, Tina Christensen, Anders H. Riis, Elizabeth E. Hatch, Lauren A. Wise, Henrik Toft Sørensen, and Kenneth J. Rothman. 2010. A successful implementation of e-epidemiology: The Danish pregnancy planning study "Snart-Gravid". *European Journal of Epidemiology* 25: 297–304.
5. Wise, Lauren A., Kenneth J. Rothman, Ellen M. Mikkelsen, Joseph B. Stanford, Amelia K. Wesselink, Craig McKinnon, Siobhan M. Gruschow, et al. 2015. Design and conduct of an Internet-based preconception cohort study in North America: Pregnancy Study Online. *Paediatric and Perinatal Epidemiology* 29: 360–371.
6. Hatch, Elizabeth E., Kristen A. Hahn, Lauren A. Wise, Ellen M. Mikkelsen, Ramya Kumar, Matthew P. Fox, Daniel R. Brooks, Anders H. Riis, Henrik Toft Sorensen, and

Kenneth J. Rothman. 2016. Evaluation of selection bias in an Internet-based study of pregnancy planners. *Epidemiology* 27: 98–104.

7. Mita, Fusami. 1984. Methed of infant feeding and postpartum amenorrhea. (Nyuji no eiyo houho to sango no amenoria). *Journal of Population Problems* 169: 43–46. (in Japanese).
8. Smith, David P. 1985. Breastfeeding, contraception, and birth intervals in developing countries. *Studies in Family Planning* 16: 154–163.
9. Iwasawa, Miho, and Fusami Mita. 2007. Delayed childbeaing and the changing age composition of women who desire children (Bansanka to Kyojikibo josei jinkou no koreika). *Journal of Population Problems* 63: 24–41. (in Japanese).
10. Ministry of Health, Labour and Welfare. 2016. Brief report on the National Nutrition Survey on preschool children, 2015 (Heisei 27 nendo nyuyoji eiyo chosa kekka no gaiyo). (in Japanese).
11. Kono, Shigemi, and Yoshikazu Watanabe. 1983. Bio-demographic conditions of fertility: An analysis of the 1981 field survey of fertility. *Journal of Population Problems* 167: 1–17. (in Japanese).
12. Tsuya, Noriko. 2009. Why does Japanese population decrease? Women, low fertility, and singlehood (Naze wagakuni no jinko wa gensho surunoka –josei, shosika, mikonka. In *Population decline and Japanese economy (Jinko gensho to nihon keizai)*, ed. Noriko Tsuya, and Yoshio Higuchi, 3–52. Tokyo: Nikkei Publishing Inc.
13. Inoue, Madoka, Colin W. Binns, Keiko Otsuka, Masamine Jimba, and Manami Matsubara. 2012. Infant feeding practices and breastfeeding duration in Japan: A review. *International Breastfeeding Journal* 7: 15. https://doi.org/10.1186/1746-4358-7-15.
14. Victora, Cesar G., Rajiv Bahl, Aluísio J.D. Barros, Giovanny V.A. França, Susan Horton, Julia Krasevec, Simon Murch, Mari Jeeva Sankar, Neff Walker, and Nigel C. Rollins. 2016. Breastfeeding in the 21st century: epidemiology, mechanisms, and lifelong effect. *The Lancet* 387: 475–490.
15. Shinoda, Tadasu. 1939. Fecundability and infertility among Japanese women (Honpou fujin no ninnyouritsu tokuni funinsho ni tsuite). *Chiryou oyobi shohou* 20: 99–103. (in Japanese).
16. Arakawa, Chikako. 2005. Effect of environmental chemical exposure on fecundity through fish consumption: A study using time to pregnancy. Dissertation, The University of Tokyo.
17. Arakawa, Chikako, Jun Yoshinaga, Kunihiro Okamura, Kunihiko Nakai, and Hiroshi Satoh. 2006. Fish consumption and time to pregnancy in Japanese women. *International Journal of Hygiene and Environmental Health* 209: 337–344.
18. Juhl, M., A.M. Nyboe Andersen, M. Grønbaek, and J. Olsen. 2001. Moderate alcohol consumption and waiting time to pregnancy. *Human Reproduction* 16: 2705–2709.
19. Tuntiseranee, P., J. Olsen, V. Chongsuvivatwong, and S. Limbutara. 1998. Fecundity in Thai and European regions: Results based on waiting time to pregnancy. *Human Reproduction* 13: 471–477. (Oxford University Press).
20. Konishi, Shoko, Soyoko Sakata, Mari S. Oba, and Kathleen A. O'Connor. Age and time to pregnancy for the first child among couples in Japan. *The Journal of Population Studies* (in press).
21. Moriki, Yoshie, Kenji Hayashi, and Rikiya Matsukura. 2015. Sexless marriages in Japan: Prevalence and reasons. In *Low fertility and reproductive health in East Asia*, ed. Naohiro Ogawa, and Iqbal H. Shah, 161–186. Dordrecht: Springer.
22. Eisenberg, Michael L., Alan W. Shindel, James F. Smith, Benjamin N. Breyer, and Larry I. Lipshultz. 2010. Socioeconomic, anthropomorphic, and demographic predictors of adult sexual activity in the United States: Data from the National Survey of Family Growth. *The Journal of Sexual Medicine* 7: 50–58.
23. Hassan, Mohamed A.M., and Stephen R. Killick. 2004. Negative lifestyle is associated with a significant reduction in fecundity. *Fertility and Sterility* 81: 384–392.
24. Rothman, Kenneth J., Lauren A. Wise, Henrik T. Sørensen, Anders H. Riis, Ellen M. Mikkelsen, and Elizabeth E. Hatch. 2013. Volitional determinants and age-related decline in fecundability: A general population prospective cohort study in Denmark. *Fertility and Sterility* 99: 1958–1964.

25. Tsukamoto, Yutaka. 1955. Actual situation of sex life among married women in agricultural villages (Noson kikonfujin seiseikatsu no jittai). *Sanfujinka no sekai* 7: 57–64. (in Japanese).
26. Sato, Ryuzaburo, and Miho Iwasawa. 2015. The sexual behavior of adolescents and young adults in Japan. In *Low fertility and reproductive health in East Asia*, ed. Naohiro Ogawa, and Iqbal H. Shah, 137–159. Dordrecht: Springer.
27. Genda, Yuji, and Atsushi Kawakami. 2006. Employment bipolarization and sexual behavior (Shugyo nikyokuka to seikodo). *Nihon rodo kenkyu zasshi* 556: 80–91. (in Japanese).
28. Wise, Lauren A., Ellen M. Mikkelsen, Kenneth J. Rothman, Anders H. Riis, Henrik Toft Sørensen, Krista F. Huybrechts, and Elizabeth E. Hatch. 2011. A prospective cohort study of menstrual characteristics and time to pregnancy. *American Journal of Epidemiology* 174: 701–709.
29. Harlow, Siobán D. 2000. Menstruation and menstrual disorders. The epidemiology of menstruation and menstrual dysfunction. In *Women and health*, ed. M.B. Goldman, and M.C. Hatch, 99–113. San Diego, CA: Academic Press.
30. Small, Chanley M., Amita K. Manatunga, Mitchel Klein, Heather S. Feigelson, Celia E. Dominguez, Ruth McChesney, and Michele Marcus. 2006. Menstrual cycle characteristics: Associations with fertility and spontaneous abortion. *Epidemiology* 17: 52–60.
31. Mutsaerts, M.A.Q., H. Groen, H.G. Huiting, W.K.H. Kuchenbecker, P.J.J. Sauer, J.A. Land, R.P. Stolk, and A. Hoek. 2012. The influence of maternal and paternal factors on time to pregnancy—A Dutch population-based birth-cohort study: The GECKO Drenthe study. *Human Reproduction* 27: 583–593.
32. Japan Society of Obstetrics and Gynecology. 2013. *Glossary of obstetrics and gynecology*. Tokyo: Japan Society of Obstetrics and Gynecology.
33. Matsumoto, Seiichi, Yasuji Nogami, and Shigeo Ohkuri. 1962. Statistical studies on menstruation; a criticism on the definition of normal menstruation. *Gunma Journal of Medical Sciences* 11: 294–318.
34. Jensen, T.K., T. Scheike, and N. Keiding. 1999. Fecundability in relation to body mass and menstrual cycle patterns. *Epidemiology* 10: 422–428.
35. Wesselink, Amelia K., Lauren A. Wise, Elizabeth E. Hatch, Kenneth J. Rothman, Ellen M. Mikkelsen, Joseph B. Stanford, Craig J. McKinnon, and Shruthi Mahalingaiah. 2016. Menstrual cycle characteristics and fecundability in a North American preconception cohort. *Annals of Epidemiology* 26: 482–487.
36. Rowland, Andrew S., Donna Day Baird, Stuart Long, Ganesa Wegienka, Siobán D. Harlow, Michael Alavanja, and Dale P. Sandler. 2002. Influence of medical conditions and lifestyle factors on the menstrual cycle. *Epidemiology* 13: 668–674.
37. Mihm, M., S. Gangooly, and S. Muttukrishna. 2011. The normal menstrual cycle in women. *Animal Reproduction Science* 124: 229–236.
38. Harlow, S.D., and S.A. Ephross. 1995. Epidemiology of menstruation and its relevance to women's health. *Epidemiologic Reviews* 17: 265–286.
39. National Institute of Population and Social Security Research. 2016. *15th Japanese national fertility survey*. Tokyo: National Institute of Population and Social Security Research.
40. Japan Family Planning Association, Inc. 2012. The 6th survey on lifestyle and awareness of men and women.
41. Raymo, J.M., and M. Iwasawa. 2008. Bridal pregnancy and spouse pairing patterns in Japan. *Journal of Marriage and Family* 70: 847–860.
42. Veltman-Verhulst, Susanne M., Edward Hughes, Reuben Olugbenga Ayeleke, and Ben J. Cohlen. 2016. Intra-uterine insemination for unexplained subfertility. In *Cochrane database of systematic reviews*, ed. Susanne M. Veltman-Verhulst. https://doi.org/10.1002/14651858.CD001838.pub5.
43. Pandian, Zabeena, Ahmed Gibreel, and Siladitya Bhattacharya. 2015. In vitro fertilisation for unexplained subfertility. In *Cochrane database of systematic reviews,* ed. Zabeena Pandian. https://doi.org/10.1002/14651858.CD003357.pub4.
44. Dyer, S., G.M. Chambers, J. de Mouzon, K.G. Nygren, F. Zegers-Hochschild, R. Mansour, O. Ishihara, M. Banker, and G.D. Adamson. 2016. International Committee for Monitoring

Assisted Reproductive Technologies world report: Assisted Reproductive Technology 2008, 2009 and 2010. *Human Reproduction* 31: 1588–1609.
45. National Institute of Population and Social Security Research. 2011. *The 14th National Fertility Survey: Summary of the couple survey*.
46. Hayashi, Reiko. 2015. Demographic impact of assisted reproductive technology (Seishoku hojo iryo no jinkougakuteki inpakuto). *Igaku no Ayumi* 254: 185–188. (in Japanese).
47. Japan Society of Obstetrics and Gynecology. 2012. ART Data Book 2012. https://plaza.umin.ac.jp/~jsog-art/2012data.pdf. Accessed 13 Oct 2017.
48. Leridon, Henri. 2004. Can assisted reproduction technology compensate for the natural decline in fertility with age? A model assessment. *Human Reproduction* 19: 1548–1553.
49. Juul, Svend, Niels Keiding, Mads Tvede, and European Infertility. 2000. Retrospectively sampled time-to-pregnancy data may make age-decreasing fecundity look increasing. *Epidemiology* 11: 717–719.
50. Steiner, Anne Z., and Anne Marie Z. Jukic. 2016. Impact of female age and nulligravidity on fecundity in an older reproductive age cohort. *Fertility and Sterility* 105: 1584–1588.
51. World Health Organization. 2016. Maternal, newborn, child and adolescent health. Stillbirths. http://www.who.int/maternal_child_adolescent/epidemiology/stillbirth/en/. Accessed 27 Sept 2016.
52. Centers for Disease Control and Prevention. 2016. Facts about Stillbirth. http://www.cdc.gov/ncbddd/stillbirth/facts.html. Accessed 27 Sept.
53. Senda, Yukiko. 2011. Increasing pregnancy attempt age and decreasing children -fertility decline as an unintended consequence. *Journal of Population Problems* 67: 22–38.
54. National Institute of Population and Social Security Research. 2016. *Marriage and Childbirth in Japan Today: The fifteenth Japanese national fertility survey, 2015 (Results of singles and married couples survey)*. Tokyo: National Institute of Population and Social Security Research. (in Japanese).
55. Sedgh, Gilda, Susheela Singh, Iqbal H. Shah, Elisabeth Ahman, Stanley K. Henshaw, and Akinrinola Bankole. 2012. Induced abortion: Incidence and trends worldwide from 1995 to 2008. *Lancet* 379: 625–632.
56. Ministry of Internal Affairs and Communications. 2015. Table 2-12 Population 15 years old and over by age group and marital status (1975–2010). http://www.stat.go.jp/data/nenkan/zuhyou/y0212000.xls. Accessed 23 Feb 2015.
57. National Institute of Population and Social Security Research. 2011. *The fourteenth Japanese National Fertility Survey in 2010: Attitudes toward marriage and family among Japanese singles (November 2011)*. Tokyo: National Institute of Population and Social Security Research. http://www.ipss.go.jp/ps-doukou/e/doukou14_s/Nfs14_Singles_Eng.pdf. Accessed 13 Oct 2017.
58. National Institute of Population and Social Security Research. 2007. Report on t*he thirteenth Japanese National Fertility Survey in 2005, volume I Marriage process and fertility of Japanese married couples*, 203–207. Tokyo: National Institute of Population and Social Security Research. (in Japanese). http://www.ipss.go.jp/syoushika/bunken/DATA/pdf/132499.pdf. Accessed 13 Oct 2017.
59. Nybo Andersen, A.M., J. Wohlfahrt, P. Christens, J. Olsen, and M. Melbye. 2000. Maternal age and fetal loss: Population based register linkage study. *BMJ* 320: 1708–1712.

Chapter 3
Exposure to Chemical Substances as a Potential Determinant Factor of Human Fertility

Jun Yoshinaga

Abstract Exposure to chemical substances has been considered a factor that affects the biological aspect of human fertility. It is widely recognized that some chemical substances have adverse effects on reproductive processes and fertility in animal models and in workers subjected to occupational exposure. Epidemiologic studies that investigate the relationship between exposure to chemical substances and time to pregnancy in occupational and environmental settings are reviewed. Occupational exposure to lead, pesticides, and solvents are suspected to decrease fecundability. Several studies report a significant association between decreased fecundability and environmental exposure to organochlorine compounds and other persistent and nonpersistent compounds; however, the results are not consistent across all studies. Exposure to chemical substances at environmental levels may not have a conspicuous effect on fecundability. However, environmental exposure is ubiquitous, and the general public is exposed on a daily basis. Even if the relative risk of environmental exposure is small, the attributable risk could be substantial because a large population is at risk. Further epidemiologic studies are warranted to elucidate the effects of environmental exposure.

Keywords Time to pregnancy · Fecundability · Chemical substance Environmental exposure · Occupational exposure

3.1 Introduction

As discussed in the preceding chapters, a better understanding of human fertility requires the differentiation of social, behavioral, biological, and other aspects of fertility and the elucidation of the relative contributions of those factors. In this chapter, one of the determinants of the biological aspect of fertility (fecundity)—namely, exposure to chemical substances—is highlighted. Epidemiologic studies on the association between occupational and environmental exposure to chemical substances and time to pregnancy (TTP), or its reciprocal, fecundability, are

S. Konishi et al., *Biodemography of Fertility in Japan*,
Population Studies of Japan, https://doi.org/10.1007/978-981-10-0176-5_3

reviewed. This study design was suggested for the first time in Baird et al. paper [1], and a number of studies have been conducted accordingly thereafter.

Numerous chemical substances are known to adversely affect one or more of the unit processes of reproduction—such as hormonal actions, spermatogenesis, reproductive cycles, or sexual behavior—in animal models. Indeed, reproductive toxicity is a routine test item in safety assessments of chemical substances. For instance, the Organization for Economic Co-operation and Development (OECD) issued the Guideline for Testing Chemicals TG 415, "One Generation Reproductive Toxicity Study" [2], for assessing the safety of chemical substances. This guideline addresses the assessment of the effects of a test chemical on male and female reproductive functions, such as gonadal function, estrous cycle, mating behavior, conception, parturition, lactation, and weaning. It was later extended to include other aspects in a new Testing Guideline, TG 443 [3].

Based on the findings in animal models, the reproductive effects of certain substances in humans were deemed to be concerning. Moreover, under occupational conditions, as will be discussed below, severe adverse effects of certain specific chemical substances on reproductive functions have been seen in human subjects. Given that exposure to such chemical substances in occupational circumstances can affect human fertility by damaging fecundity, the question was raised whether similar effects could occur in nonoccupational environmental circumstances with lower exposure levels.

3.2 Occupational Exposure and Fertility

In an occupational setting, it is generally understood that people (workers) are exposed to higher doses of specific and/or mixtures of chemical substances than they are in environmental conditions. In this regard, findings in occupational epidemiology are helpful in assessing the health hazards and/or risks of these substances in humans. Therefore, occupational epidemiology studies provide significant insight into hazard/risk assessment of these substances for the general population.

Certain chemical substances were known in the past to adversely affect human reproductive functions. A soil nematocide, 1,2-dibromo-3-chloropropane (DBCP), is a typical and classic example. In 1977, azoospermia and oligospermia, as well as elevated serum FSH and LH, were found among pesticide production workers exposed to DBCP who experienced infertility problems [4, 5]. Lead is another well-known substance that can adversely affect male and female reproductive functions through occupational exposure.

Snijder et al. [6] published an extensive review of the association between occupational exposure to chemical substances and TTP. Table 3.1 summarizes the results of the occupational epidemiology studies compiled by Snijder et al. with respect to exposure indices (occupation, mixture of chemical substances, or specific

Table 3.1 Number of occupational epidemiology studies in which a significantly deviated fecundability ratio (FR)[a] was observed

Exposure index	FR > 1	NS[b]	FR < 1	Total
Occupation	0	18	10	28
Chemical mixture	0	2	0	2
Specific chemical	0	9	6	15
Total	0	29	16	45

Based on the occupational epidemiology studies compiled by Snijder et al. [6]

[a]FR is the ratio of the fecundability of an exposed (or more exposed) population to the fecundability of a reference (nonexposed or less exposed) population

[b]Not significantly different from 1

substance) and fecundability ratio (FR). FR is the ratio of the fecundability of an exposed (or more exposed) population to that of an unexposed (or less exposed) population. Of the 45 studies compiled, nonsignificant FR was observed in 29 studies, and significantly decreased FR was found in 16 studies. No study reported significantly elevated FR. Although publication bias must be considered, this compilation suggests at the very least that certain occupations and/or exposure to chemicals at occupational levels can significantly reduce human fecundability (or prolong TTP).

Occupations associated with significantly decreased FR include greenhouse workers (male), fruit growers (male), flower production workers (female), hairdressers (female), nurses (female), semiconductor manufacturers (female), farmers (couples), and industry workers (couples) [7–15]. Chemical substances for which exposure was associated with decreased FR include lead and solvents [16–21]. In particular, occupations that could be associated with exposure to pesticides and/or herbicides or to solvents and lead were suggested to be related to decreased FR. In fact, Snjider et al. [6] concluded that pesticides and lead are suggestive of chemicals or groups of chemicals that are of concern for human reproduction (solvents were not mentioned in this regard, for unknown reasons).

The apparent shortcomings of existing occupational epidemiology studies include an absence of information on the specific chemical substance(s) that may actually affect human reproduction. This shortcoming is particularly evident in studies in which occupations or job titles are used as an exposure index. Although pesticides (and solvents, according to the present author) were identified based on the literature review of occupational epidemiology, the specific chemical substance (s) in those chemical groups that may affect FR remain unknown. In contrast, with regard to lead, a dose-effect relationship was proposed; specifically, a significantly decreased FR was associated with whole blood lead >30 μg/dL and especially >40 μg/dL (Fig. 3.1). This information is extremely important, not only in the occupational health field but also in the reproductive risk assessment of lead, because the general population is nonoccupationally exposed to lead in everyday life.

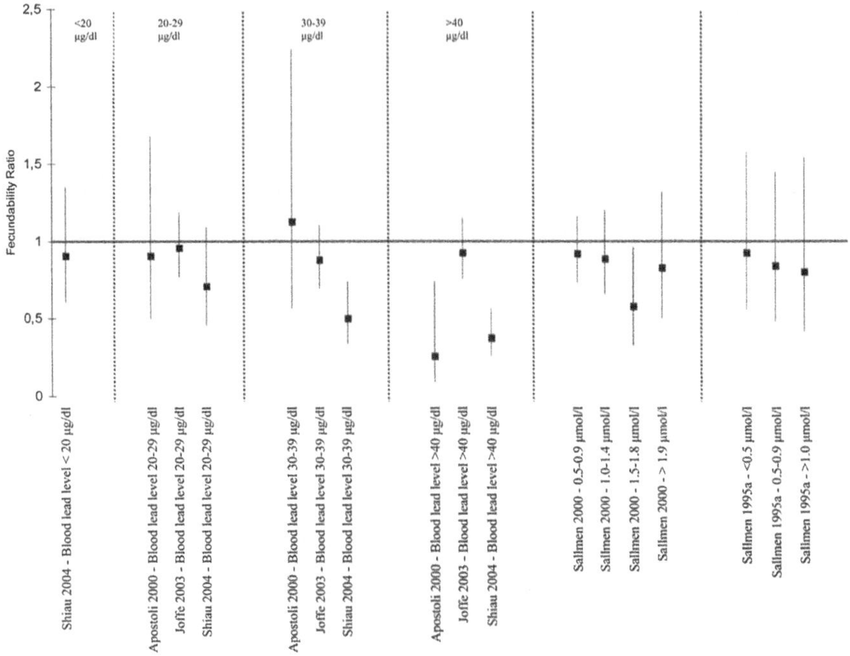

Fig. 3.1 Forest plot showing dose-effect relations between blood lead concentration and TTP. Reproduced with permission from Snijder et al. [6]

3.3 Environmental Exposure and Fertility

The TTP of couples in the general population has been investigated in relation to nonoccupational exposure to chemical substances. The chemical substances of interest with respect to the fecundity of general populations included both persistent and nonpersistent compounds. Persistent compounds typically include organochlorine (OC) compounds, such as polychlorinated biphenyl (PCB), OC pesticides, and dioxins, whereas nonpersistent compounds include phthalate esters (PE). These chemical substances are known to mimic the activities of endogenous hormones in in vitro assays and animal models and thus have been labeled endocrine-disrupting chemicals (EDC). Moreover, the general public is more or less exposed to these chemicals in everyday life through diet, consumer products, indoor environments, and other means. Therefore, the possible adverse effects of these substances on fecundity have been investigated.

3.3.1 Persistent Chemical Substances

Exposure of the general population to persistent chemical substances occurs primarily through diet, particularly fish consumption. This is because (1) the biological half-lives of these substances are long, due to their lipophilic nature and slow metabolism, and (2) fish situate at higher trophic levels in the aquatic ecosystem and therefore contain these substances at higher concentrations due to the biomagnification (extension of bioconcentration along the food chain) effect.

Early studies on exposure to persistent chemical substances and TTP used fish consumption as an exposure index [22–25], most likely because fish consumption is easily assessed with questionnaire surveys. These studies focused on OCs, including PCBs, OC pesticides, and others. Among these studies, significantly decreased FR in women who consumed more fish (as estimated by the duration and frequency of consumption) was found in only one study, which concluded that more frequent fish eaters had FR = 0.75 (95% CI: 0.59–0.91) and that those with 3–6 years of fish consumption had FR = 0.73 (0.54–0.98) [24].

Apparently, the frequency/duration of fish consumption by test subjects is a surrogate but inaccurate measure of specific substances, which could lead to the misclassification of exposure and seriously obscure the relationship, if one is present. Therefore, recent studies employ concentration of OCs and other substances in the blood of subjects to evaluate the association with TTP or FR and to obtain more accurate exposure measures. Four such studies regarding OCs (PCBs and/or PCBs and OC pesticides) are available [26–29]. In these studies, blood was taken from female subjects before or during pregnancy, and serum OC concentrations were measured. The concentrations were then related to TTP or FR by regression analysis. The analytical methods (e.g., total concentration or congener-specific concentrations of PCB) and statistical methods (multiple regression, logistic regression, or the Cox proportional hazard model) differ across studies. A significantly decreased FR in subjects with higher blood concentrations of PCB and DDE (a metabolite of DDT, an OC pesticide) was found in the most recent study, which used the most sophisticated analytical method [29], but not in other studies. In the most recent study, which was a French study, the fecundability OR was 0.56 (95% CI 0.37–0.85) for the group with the highest serum PCB concentration (sum of ten congeners: >0.410 μg/L) when the group with the lowest concentration (<0.266 μg/L) was used as reference after controlling for potential confounders.

Dioxins are another group of OC compounds of interest in the fecundity field because of their high reproductive toxicity. Eskenazi et al. [30] measured the concentration of 2,3,7,8-tetrachloro-dibenzo-*p*-dioxin (TCDD) in the stored serum of 278 women who resided in an area contaminated with dioxins due to the Seveso accident in 1976 (an explosion of an OC pesticide-manufacturing plant emitted dioxins, resulting in excessive exposure for residents living near the plant) and who had attempted pregnancy after the accident and related these data to TTP. A statistically significant dose-dependent decrease of fecundability OR was obtained. OR generally increased and a portion of the significant results diminished when TCDD concentrations at the time of the explosion were replaced with those estimated for the period of attempted conception; however, the relation remained significant when serum TCDD concentrations were used in the model as a continuous variable (Table 3.2). Based on this relationship, it was estimated that a tenfold increase of serum TCDD was associated with a 27% decrease in FR. Although the subjects of this study were exposed to excessive levels of TCDD as a result of the accident and thus had higher serum TCDD concentrations after the accident, the estimated serum TCDD concentrations during attempted conception were close to the average value of European populations. Therefore, the authors suggested that TCDD exposure levels of the general population may reduce fecundity [30].

In addition to OC compounds, increased serum levels of polybrominated diphenyl ethers (PBDEs) were found to be significantly associated with decreased FR in 223 female Mexican immigrants in California [31]. PBDEs are a group of flame retardants widely used in carpets, furniture, textiles, and plastics; due to their common usage, the general public is exposed to PBDEs primarily through indoor environments. The

Table 3.2 Association between serum TCDD concentration and TTP in Italian women who attempted pregnancy after the Seveso accident

	N	Crude fecundability OR (95% CI)	Adjusted fecundability OR[a] (95% CI)
Serum TCDD concentration[b] at the time of explosion[c]			
(Continuous; $\log_{10}$TCDD)	278	0.81 (0.65–1.02)	0.75 (0.60–0.95)
Categorical			
<20	52	1.00	1.00
20.1-44.4	76	0.96 (0.61–1.52)	0.81 (0.52–1.05)
44.5-100	75	0.88 (0.57–1.36)	0.71 (0.46–1.09)
100<	75	0.76 (0.50–1.16)	0.63 (0.42–0.96)
Estimated serum TCDD concentration during conception attempt[d]			
(Continuous; $\log_{10}$TCDD)	278	0.77 (0.61–0.96)	0.73 (0.58–0.94)
Categorical			
<6.0	52	1.00	1.00
6.1–14.2	76	1.45 (0.95–2.22)	1.49 (0.95–2.33)
14.3–40.7	75	1.00 (0.66–1.52)	0.95 (0.61–1.47)
40.8<	75	0.79 (0.53–1.17)	0.76 (0.49–1.17)

This table was reproduced from Eskenazi et al. [30] and partly modified by the present author

[a]Adjusted for parity, maternal/paternal ages, irregular menstrual cycles, oral contraceptive use, smoking, and history of gynecologic or chronic health conditions

[b]Expressed as pg/g fat

[c]Measured concentration of TCDD in serum samples obtained immediately after the Seveso accident in 1976

[d]Serum TCDD concentration of subject during conception attempt. Estimated for each subject based on measured concentration, time elapsed from explosion to conception attempt, and reported biological half-life of TCDD (9 years)

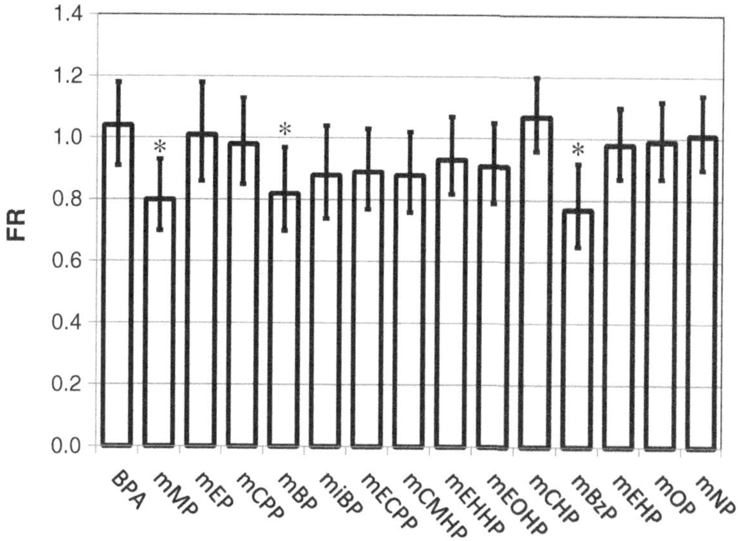

Fig. 3.2 Urinary phthalate metabolite concentrations of males and fecundability odds ratios of couples with 95% confidence interval. Prepared based on Buck-Louis et al. [35]. An asterisk in the figure denotes significance at $p < 0.05$

implication of this study lies in the fact that a significant association was observed in subjects with serum PBDE concentration ranges that were similar to those of the general population of Mexican immigrants in the USA. A ten-fold increase of the serum concentrations of four major congeners (BDE-47, -99, -100, and -153) and/or the sum of the congeners yielded a 24–48% decrease in FR.

Organic fluorine compounds, such as perfluorooctanoate (PFOA) and perfluorooctane sulfonate (PFOS), are "emerging" persistent compounds; they are used in certain industries and consumer products (such as paper wraps and textiles) and in pesticides. Biological monitoring programs frequently detect PFOS and PFOA in blood and urine, demonstrating widespread exposure of the general population. PFOA and PFOS levels in serum were associated with TTP in three studies conducted in Denmark [32–34]. In the first study [32], increased serum concentrations of PFOS and PFOA were associated with increased OR of conception delay (TTP > 12 months) and with decreased fecundability OR (0.67–0.74 for PFOS and 0.60–0.73 for PFOA). However, these relations were not confirmed in the other studies (Fig. 3.2).

3.3.2 Nonpersistent Chemical Substances

A number of nonpersistent compounds with short biological half-lives have also raised concerns relating to their endocrine disrupting activities and the potential resultant adverse effects on fecundity. Although they have short biological half-lives, if exposure to these compounds is persistent or frequent (i.e., several times per day), then a certain amount is expected to be present in the body.

Phthalate esters (PEs) are a group of compounds frequently used to plasticize resins, such as polyvinyl chloride (PVC), to make the resins flexible. Because PVCs and other plastic products are abundant in our daily lives—as building materials, consumer products, or food wraps—we are frequently and abundantly exposed to PEs and other plasticizers. Certain PEs are known to exhibit anti-androgenic activity, which raises concerns about whether they can affect fecundity by damaging male reproductive functions. Recently, Buck-Louis et al. [35] found significantly decreased FR in female subjects whose partners had higher urinary metabolite concentrations of certain PEs (Fig. 3.3). It is noteworthy that increased urinary metabolite concentrations of (1) butyl benzyl phthalate (BBzP) and di-n-butyl phthalate (DBP) and (2) mono benzyl phthalate (mBzP) and mono butyl phthalate (mBP) were associated with significantly decreased FR because these two PEs are known anti-androgenic compounds. Several epidemiologic studies showed significant negative associations between the urinary mBP or mBzP concentration of male subjects and semen quality [36, 37]. However, later studies failed to find that increased concentrations of PE metabolites in urine or serum were associated with decreased FR [38, 39].

In Vélez et al. [39], a significantly decreased FR was observed in female subjects with higher urinary triclosan concentration. Triclosan is a known EDC with estrogenic activity and is added to personal care products (PCPs), such as soap and toothpaste, as an antiseptic. The general public is thus exposed to triclosan through the use of these PCP products.

As shown in this section, the association between exposure to persistent and nonpersistent chemical substances and TTP has been found to be significant in certain studies but not in many others. These equivocal results may be due to

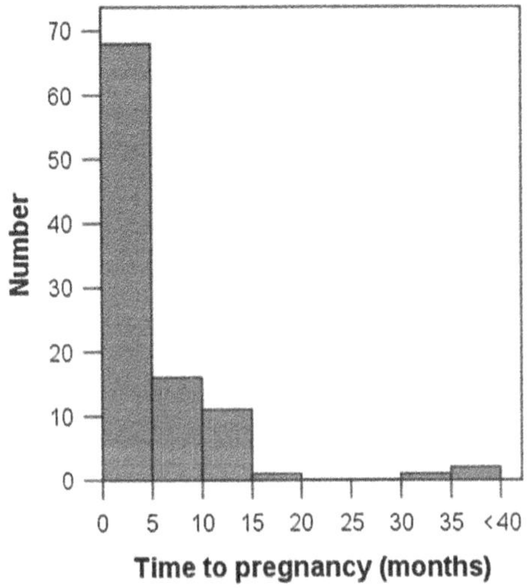

Fig. 3.3 Distribution of time to pregnancy of Japanese women (n = 109) recorded during index pregnancy. The subjects were recruited from the gynecology department of a university hospital in Kyushu, Japan

Table 3.3 List of chemical substances to which exposure at environmental levels is suspected to adversely affect fecundity

Chemical substances	Persistent/ nonpersistent	Usage/Exposure source for the general public
PCB	P	Fish consumption
DDT	P	Fish consumption
Dioxins	P	Fish consumption
PBDE	P	Indoor environment (flame retardant)
PFOS/PFOA	P	Fish consumption
Phthalate esters	NP	Indoor environment, food wrapping, etc.
Triclosan	NP	Personal care products (antiseptic)

relatively small sample sizes, exposure misclassification due to the improper selection of exposure measures, lower exposure levels, and other factors. The chemical substances discussed in this review are those that the general public is exposed to on a daily basis through diet and other proximate environmental factors (Table 3.3). This exposure means that the population at risk is substantial, and thus even the smallest effect of a substance may have serious implications for fecundity at a population level. Therefore, the accumulation of results from well-designed studies is warranted.

3.4 Environmental Exposure-TTP Study in Japan

Only two studies examine the relationship between exposure to chemical substances and TTP in Japan. Arakawa et al. [40] examined the possible relationship between hair mercury levels and TTP in 193 women in Sendai, Japan, during 2002–2004. In this study, the use of hair mercury concentration had two purposes: One was to assess the possible effect of mercury itself on fecundity, and the other was to use mercury as a surrogate for fish consumption. Hair mercury levels were not significantly associated with reported TTP, suggesting that fish consumption does not affect fecundity.

The second study is a partially unpublished work by the present author [41]. Dioxin concentration in the breast milk of the mothers of newborns was related to TTP in the southern part of Japan in 2004–2005. In this study, 153 pregnant women (gestational week 20<) were approached at the gynecology department of a university hospital, and TTP was obtained from 109 mothers through a questionnaire administered during pregnancy. Breast milk was obtained from 48 of the 109 mothers at 30 days postpartum and subjected to an analysis of seven congeners of polychlorinated dibenzodioxins (PCDDs), ten congeners of polychlorinated dibenzofurans (PCDFs), and 12 coplanar PCBs. The method used was gas chromatography–high-resolution mass spectrometry preceded by extraction and purification, which is consistent with the official method of the Japanese government. The subjects were divided into two groups based on reported TTP: those who had ≤ 6 months TTP and those who had ≥ 7 months. A Cox regression analysis was conducted using dioxin concentrations in breast milk as an independent variable along with other covariates. The average concentration of dioxin expressed as a toxicity equivalent concentration was 10.5 pg TEQ/g fat, indicating that the mothers in the study had body burdens of dioxin similar to those of the general population in Japan at that time. Figure 3.4 shows the TTP distribution of

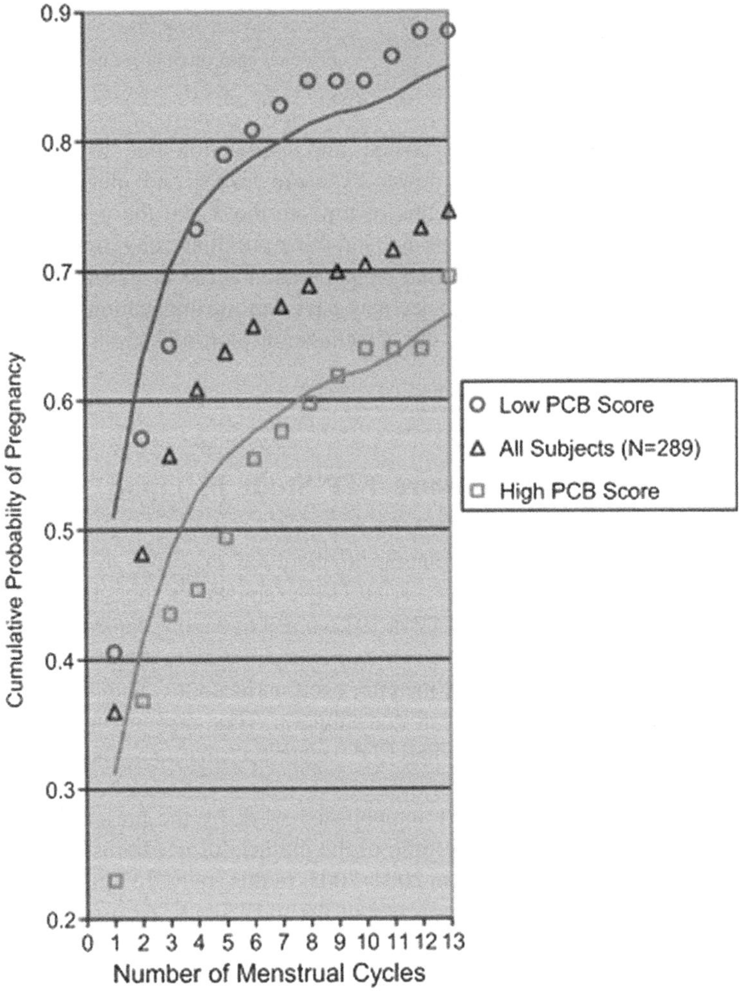

Fig. 3.4 Cumulative probability of pregnancy after 13 menstrual cycles for 289 daughters according to the PCB concentrations detected in their mothers' preserved serum. Low PCB score and High PCB score denote daughters whose mothers had low levels (<25 percentile) and high levels (>75 percentile) of serum PCB concentration, respectively. Reproduced with permission from Cohn et al. [49]

Table 3.4 Results of Cox regression on time to pregnancy and demographic and lifestyle factors and breast milk dioxin concentration in Japanese women ($n = 48$)

	Adjusted hazard ratio	95% CI	P value
BMI (kg/m^2)	1.34	0.97–1.83	0.07
Parity	0.84	0.54–1.30	0.43
Age	1.15	0.74–1.77	0.53
Frequency of intercourse (%)			
<1/week	1.00		0.58
1/week	0.80	0.33–1.92	0.61
>2/week	0.52	0.15–1.81	0.30
Milk consumption (glass/w)	0.90	0.58–1.38	0.62
Caffeine intake (mg/w)	1.04	0.66–1.64	0.87
Alcohol intake (g/w)	0.76	0.45–1.29	0.31
Meat consumption (times/w)	1.01	0.59–1.70	0.98
Smoking	1.34	0.53–3.36	0.54
Total dioxin concentration in breast milk (pg TEQ/g fat)	0.77	0.48–1.23	0.27

the subjects, and Table 3.4 shows the result of logistic regression analysis. None of the variables, including breast milk dioxin concentration, was significantly related to TTP. The small sample size was a serious hindrance to detecting a small effect, if any, of low-level dioxin exposure; in fact, the exposure levels of dioxin (expressed as whole blood concentration) of the general Japanese population around 2005 were 20 pg TEQ/g fat [42], which corresponds to 40 pg TEQ/g serum. As seen in Table 3.2, the results for Seveso residents show that an effect on FR was not detectable in subjects with 40 pg TCDD/g fat. [The Seveso result was expressed as pg TCDD/g serum fat, which included only TCDD; however, other PCDDs and PCDFs also contribute to the harmful effects of dioxins. In this regard, 40 pg TEQ/g fat (Japanese result) indicates lower exposure levels than 40 pg TCDD/g fat (Seveso result)].

To date, studies on the effects of exposure to chemical substances on TTP remain scarce in Japan. However, the Japanese are among the greatest consumers of fish and fish products in the world; therefore, they are exposed to high levels of persistent pollutants, including OC compounds and brominated, fluorinated, and other types of compounds, via their daily diet. Further studies using larger sample sizes are warranted to investigate the effects of chemical substance exposure on fecundity.

20. Wennborg, H., L. Bodin, H. Vainio, and G. Axelsson. 2001. Solvent use and time to pregnancy among female personnel in biomedical laboratories in Sweden. *Occupational and Environmental Medicine* 58: 225–231.
21. Shiau, C.-Y., J.-D. Wang, and P.-C. Chen. 2004. Decreased fecundity among male lead workers. *Occupational and Environmental Medicine* 61: 915–923.
22. Buck, G.M., L.E. Sever, P. Mendola, M. Zielezny, and J.E. Vena. 1997. Consumption of contaminated sport fish from Lake Ontario and time-to-pregnancy. New York State Angler Cohort. *American Journal of Epidemiology* 146: 949–954.
23. Buck, G.M., P. Mendola, J.E. Vena, L.E. Sever, P. Kostyniak, H. Greizerstein, J. Olson, and F.D. Stephen. 1999. Paternal Lake Ontario fish consumption and risk of conception delay, New York State Angler Cohort. *Environmental Research, Section A* 80: S13–S18.
24. Buck, G.M., J.E. Vena, E.F. Schisterman, J. Dmochowski, P. Mendola, L.E. Sever, E. Fitzgerald, P. Kostyniak, H. Greizerstein, and J. Olson. 2000. Parental consumption of contaminated sport fish from Lake Ontario and predicted fecundability. *Epidemiology* 11: 388–393.
25. Axmon, A., L. Rylander, U. Strömberg, and L. Hagmar. 2002. Female fertility in relation to the consumption of fish contaminated with persistent organochlorine compounds. *Scandinavian Journal of Work, Environment & Health* 28: 124–132.
26. Axmon, A., L. Rylander, U. Strömberg, B. Jönsson, P. Nilsson-Ehle, and L. Hagmar. 2004. Polychlorinated biphenyls in serum and time to pregnancy. *Environmental Research* 96: 186–195.
27. Gesink Law, D.C., M.A. Klebanoff, J.W. Brock, D.B. Dunson, and M.P. Longnecker. 2005. Maternal serum levels of polychlorinated biphenyls and 1,1-dichloro-2,2-bis(*p*-chlorophenyl) ethylene (DDE) and time to pregnancy. *American Journal of Epidemiology* 162: 523–532.
28. Buck-Luois, G.M., J. Dmochowski, C. Lynch, P. Kostyniak, B.M. McGuinness, and J.E. Vena. 2009. Polychlorinated biphenyl serum concentrations, lifestyle and time-to-pregnancy. *Human Reproduction* 24: 451–458.
29. Chevrier, C., C. Warembourg, E. Gaudreau, C. Monfort, A. Le Blanc, L. Guldner, and S. Cordier. 2013. Organochlorine pesticides, polychlorinated biphenyls, seafood consumption, and time-to-pregnancy. *Epidemiology* 24: 251–260.
30. Eskenazi, B., M. Warner, A.R. Marks, S. Samuels, L. Needham, P. Brambilla, and P. Mocarelli. 2010. Serum dioxin concentrations and time to pregnancy. *Epidemiology* 21: 224–231.
31. Harley, K.G., A.R. Marks, J. Chevrier, A. Bradman, A. Sjödin, and B. Eskenazi. 2010. PBDE concentrations in women's serum and fecundability. *Environmental Health Perspectives* 118: 699–704.
32. Fei, C., J.K. McLaughlin, L. Lipworth, and J. Olsen. 2009. Maternal levels of perfluorinated chemicals and subfecundity. *Human Reproduction* 1: 1–6.
33. Vestergaard, S., F. Nielsen, A.-M. Andersson, N.H. Hjøllund, P. Grandjean, H.R. Andersen, and T.K. Jensen. 2012. Association between perfluorinated compounds and time to pregnancy in a prospective cohort of Danish couples attempting to conceive. *Human Reproduction* 27: 873–880.
34. Jørgensen, K.T., I.O. Specht, V. Lenters, C.C. Bach, L. Rylander, B.A.G. Jönsson, C.H. Lindh, A. Giwercman, D. Heederik, G. Toft, and J.P. Bonde. 2014. Perfluoroalkyl substances and time to pregnancy in couples from Greenland. *Poland and Ukraine. Environmental Health* 13: 116.
35. Buck-Louis, G.M., R. Sundaram, A.M. Sweeney, E.F. Schisterman, J. Maisog, and K. Kannan. 2014. Urinary bisphenol A, phthalates, and couple fecundity: the Longitudinal Investigation of Fertility and the Environment (LIFE) Study. *Fertility and Sterility* 101: 1359–1366.
36. Duty, S.M., M.J. Silva, D.B. Barr, J.W. Brock, L. Ryan, Z. Chen, R.F. Herrick, D.C. Christiani, and R. Hauser. 2003. Phthalate exposure and human semen parameters. *Epidemiology* 14: 269–277.

References

1. Baird, D.D., A.J. Wilcox, and C.R. Weinberg. 1986. Use of time to pregnancy to study environmental exposure. *American Journal of Epidemiology* 124: 470–480.
2. OECD. 1983. Test No. 415: One-generation reproduction toxicity study. http://www.oecd-ilibrary.org/environment/test-no-415-one-generation-reproduction-toxicity-study_9789264070844-en. Accessed 12 Sept 2016.
3. OECD. 2012. Test No. 443: Extended one-generation reproductive toxicity study. http://www.oecd-ilibrary.org/environment/test-no-443-extended-one-generation-reproductive-toxicity-study_9789264185371-en. Accessed 12 Sept 2016.
4. Whorton, D., R.M. Krauss, S. Marshall, and T.H. Milby. 1977. Infertility in male pesticide workers. *Lancet* 2: 1259–1261.
5. Whorton, D., T.H. Milby, R.M. Krauss, and H.A. Stubbs. 1979. Testicular function in DBCP exposed pesticide workers. *Journal of Occupational Medicine* 21: 161–166.
6. Snijder, C.A., E. Velde, N. Roeleveld, and A. Burdorf. 2012. Occupational exposure to chemical substances and time to pregnancy: A systematic review. *Human Reproduction Update* 18: 284–300.
7. de Cock, J., K. Westveer, D. Heederik, E. te Velde, and R. van Kooij. 1994. Time to pregnancy and occupational exposure to pesticides in fruit growers in The Netherlands. *Occupational and Environmental Medicine* 51: 693–699.
8. Spinelli, A., I. Figà-Talamanca, and J. Osborn. 1997. Time to pregnancy and occupation in a group of Italian women. *International Journal of Epidemiology* 26: 601–609.
9. Plenge-Bonig, A., and W. Karmaus. 1999. Exposure to toluene in the printing industry is associated with subfecundity in women but not in men. *Occupational and Environmental Medicine* 56: 443–448.
10. Chen, P.-C., G.-Y. Hsieh, J.-D. Wang, and T.-J. Cheng. 2002. Prolonged time to pregnancy in female workers exposed to ethylene glycol ethers in semiconductor manufacturing. *Epidemiology* 13: 191–196.
11. Fransman, W., N. Roeleveld, S. Peelen, W. de Kort, H. Kromhout, and D. Heederik. 2007. Nurses with dermal exposure to antineoplastic drugs: Reproductive outcomes. *Epidemiology* 18: 112–119.
12. Idorovo, A.J., L.H. Sanin, D. Cole, J. Chavarro, H. Caceres, J. Narvaez, and M. Restrepo. 2005. Time to first pregnancy among women working in agricultural production. *International Archives of Occupational and Environmental Health* 78: 493–500.
13. Axmon, A., L. Rylander, L. Lillienberg, M. Albin, and L. Hagmar. 2006. Fertility among female hairdressers. *Scandinavian Journal of Work, Environment & Health* 32: 51–60.
14. Bretveld, R., S. Kik, M. Hooiveld, I. van Rooij, G. Zielhuis, and N. Roeleveld. 2008. Time-to-pregnancy among male greenhouse workers. *Occupational and Environmental Medicine* 65: 185–190.
15. Harley, K.G., A.R. Marks, A. Bradman, D.B. Barr, and B. Eskenazi. 2008. DDT exposure, work in agriculture, and time to pregnancy among farmworkers in California. *Journal of Occupational and Environmental Medicine* 50: 1335–1342.
16. Sallmén, M., A. Anttila, M.-L. Lindbohm, P. Kyyrönen, H. Taskinen, and K. Hemminki. 1995. Time to pregnancy among women occupationally exposed to lead. *Journal of Occupational and Environmental Medicine* 37: 931–934.
17. Sallmén, M., M.-L. Lindbohm, A. Anttila, P. Kyyrönen, H. Taskinen, E. Nykyri, and K. Hemminki. 1998. Time to pregnancy among the wives of men exposed to organic solvent. *Occupational and Environmental Medicine* 55: 24–30.
18. Sallmén, M., M. Neto, and O.N. Mayan. 2008. Reduced fertility among shoe manufacturing workers. *Occupational and Environmental Medicine* 65: 518–524.
19. Apostoli, P., A. Bellini, S. Porru, and L. Bisanti. 2000. The effect of lead on male fertility: A time to pregnancy (TTP) study. *American Journal of Industrial Medicine* 38: 310–315.

20. Wennborg, H., L. Bodin, H. Vainio, and G. Axelsson. 2001. Solvent use and time to pregnancy among female personnel in biomedical laboratories in Sweden. *Occupational and Environmental Medicine* 58: 225–231.
21. Shiau, C.-Y., J.-D. Wang, and P.-C. Chen. 2004. Decreased fecundity among male lead workers. *Occupational and Environmental Medicine* 61: 915–923.
22. Buck, G.M., L.E. Sever, P. Mendola, M. Zielezny, and J.E. Vena. 1997. Consumption of contaminated sport fish from Lake Ontario and time-to-pregnancy. New York State Angler Cohort. *American Journal of Epidemiology* 146: 949–954.
23. Buck, G.M., P. Mendola, J.E. Vena, L.E. Sever, P. Kostyniak, H. Greizerstein, J. Olson, and F.D. Stephen. 1999. Paternal Lake Ontario fish consumption and risk of conception delay, New York State Angler Cohort. *Environmental Research, Section A* 80: S13–S18.
24. Buck, G.M., J.E. Vena, E.F. Schisterman, J. Dmochowski, P. Mendola, L.E. Sever, E. Fitzgerald, P. Kostyniak, H. Greizerstein, and J. Olson. 2000. Parental consumption of contaminated sport fish from Lake Ontario and predicted fecundability. *Epidemiology* 11: 388–393.
25. Axmon, A., L. Rylander, U. Strömberg, and L. Hagmar. 2002. Female fertility in relation to the consumption of fish contaminated with persistent organochlorine compounds. *Scandinavian Journal of Work, Environment & Health* 28: 124–132.
26. Axmon, A., L. Rylander, U. Strömberg, B. Jönsson, P. Nilsson-Ehle, and L. Hagmar. 2004. Polychlorinated biphenyls in serum and time to pregnancy. *Environmental Research* 96: 186–195.
27. Gesink Law, D.C., M.A. Klebanoff, J.W. Brock, D.B. Dunson, and M.P. Longnecker. 2005. Maternal serum levels of polychlorinated biphenyls and 1,1-dichloro-2,2-bis(*p*-chlorophenyl) ethylene (DDE) and time to pregnancy. *American Journal of Epidemiology* 162: 523–532.
28. Buck-Luois, G.M., J. Dmochowski, C. Lynch, P. Kostyniak, B.M. McGuinness, and J.E. Vena. 2009. Polychlorinated biphenyl serum concentrations, lifestyle and time-to-pregnancy. *Human Reproduction* 24: 451–458.
29. Chevrier, C., C. Warembourg, E. Gaudreau, C. Monfort, A. Le Blanc, L. Guldner, and S. Cordier. 2013. Organochlorine pesticides, polychlorinated biphenyls, seafood consumption, and time-to-pregnancy. *Epidemiology* 24: 251–260.
30. Eskenazi, B., M. Warner, A.R. Marks, S. Samuels, L. Needham, P. Brambilla, and P. Mocarelli. 2010. Serum dioxin concentrations and time to pregnancy. *Epidemiology* 21: 224–231.
31. Harley, K.G., A.R. Marks, J. Chevrier, A. Bradman, A. Sjödin, and B. Eskenazi. 2010. PBDE concentrations in women's serum and fecundability. *Environmental Health Perspectives* 118: 699–704.
32. Fei, C., J.K. McLaughlin, L. Lipworth, and J. Olsen. 2009. Maternal levels of perfluorinated chemicals and subfecundity. *Human Reproduction* 1: 1–6.
33. Vestergaard, S., F. Nielsen, A.-M. Andersson, N.H. Hjøllund, P. Grandjean, H.R. Andersen, and T.K. Jensen. 2012. Association between perfluorinated compounds and time to pregnancy in a prospective cohort of Danish couples attempting to conceive. *Human Reproduction* 27: 873–880.
34. Jørgensen, K.T., I.O. Specht, V. Lenters, C.C. Bach, L. Rylander, B.A.G. Jönsson, C.H. Lindh, A. Giwercman, D. Heederik, G. Toft, and J.P. Bonde. 2014. Perfluoroalkyl substances and time to pregnancy in couples from Greenland. *Poland and Ukraine. Environmental Health* 13: 116.
35. Buck-Louis, G.M., R. Sundaram, A.M. Sweeney, E.F. Schisterman, J. Maisog, and K. Kannan. 2014. Urinary bisphenol A, phthalates, and couple fecundity: the Longitudinal Investigation of Fertility and the Environment (LIFE) Study. *Fertility and Sterility* 101: 1359–1366.
36. Duty, S.M., M.J. Silva, D.B. Barr, J.W. Brock, L. Ryan, Z. Chen, R.F. Herrick, D.C. Christiani, and R. Hauser. 2003. Phthalate exposure and human semen parameters. *Epidemiology* 14: 269–277.

37. Hauser, R., J.D. Meeker, S. Duty, M.J. Silva, and A.M. Calafat. 2006. Altered semen quality in relation to urinary concentrations of phthalate monoester and oxidative metabolites. *Epidemiology* 17: 682–691.
38. Specht, I.O., J.P. Bonde, G. Toft, C.H. Lindh, B.A.G. Jönsson, and K.T. Jørgensen. 2015. Serum phthalate levels and time to pregnancy in couples from Greenland, Poland and Ukraine. *PLoS ONE*. https://doi.org/10.1371/journal.pone.0120070.
39. Vélez, M.P., T.E. Arbuckle, and W.D. Fraser. 2015. Female exposure to phenols and phthalates and time to pregnancy: The Maternal-Infant Research on Environmental Chemicals (MIREC) study. *Fertility and Sterility* 103: 1011–1020.
40. Arakawa, C., J. Yoshinaga, K. Okamura, K. Nakai, and H. Sato. 2006. Fish consumption and time to pregnancy in Japanese women. *International Journal of Hygiene and Environmental Health* 209: 337–344.
41. Arakawa, C., J. Yoshinaga, K. Kitamura, S. Hashimoto, H. Imai, and T. Kato. 2007. The relationship between dioxins exposure and female fecundity. A time to pregnancy study (Daiokishin-rui bakuro ni yoru ninyouryoku heno eikyou—jyutai machijikan chousahou ni yoru kentou). *Japanese. Journal of Hygiene* 62: 442. (in Japanese).
42. Ministry of the Environment, Japan. 2012. The exposure to dioxins and other chemical compounds in the Japanese people. http://www.env.go.jp/chemi/dioxin/pamph/cd/en_full.pdf. Accessed 13 Sept 2016.
43. Swan, S.H., K.M. Main, F. Liu, S.L. Stewart, R.L. Kruse, A.M. Carafat, C.S. Mao, J.B. Redmon, C.L. Ternand, S. Sullivan, J. Lynn Teague, and the Study for Future Families Research Team. 2005. Decrease in anogenital distance among male infants with prenatal phthalate exposure. *Environmental Health Perspectives* 113: 1056–1061.
44. Huang, P.-C., P.-L. Kuo, Y.-Y. Chou, S.-J. Lin, and C.-C. Lee. 2012. Association between prenatal exposure to phthalates and the health of newborns. *Environment International* 35: 14–20.
45. Suzuki, Y., J. Yoshinaga, Y. Mizumoto, S. Serizawa, and H. Shiraishi. 2012. Foetal exposure to phthalate esters and anogenital distance in male newborns. *International Journal of Andrology* 35: 236–244.
46. Eisenberg, M.L., M.H. Hsieh, R. Chanc Walters, R. Lrasnow, and L.I. Lipshultz. 2011. The relationship between anogenital distance, fatherhood, and fertility in adult men. *PLoS ONE* 6: e18973.
47. Eisenberg, M.L., M. Shy, R. Chanc Walters, and L.I. Lipshultz. 2012. The relationship between anogenital distance and azoospermia in adult male. *International Journal of Andrology* 35: 1–5.
48. Cohn, B.A., P.M. Cirillo, M.S. Wolff, P.J. Schwingl, R.D. Cohen, R.I. Sholtz, A. Ferrara, R.E. Chiristianson, B.J. van den Berg, and P.K. Siiteri. 2003. DDT and DDE exposure in mothers and time to pregnancy in daughters. *Lancet* 361: 2205–2206.
49. Cohn, B.A., P.M. Cirillo, R.I. Sholtz, A. Ferrara, J.-S. Park, and P.J. Schwingl. 2011. Polychlorinated biphenyl (PCB) exposure in mothers and time to pregnancy in daughters. *Reproductive Toxicology* 31: 290–296.

Chapter 4
Directions for Future Research

Shoko Konishi, Emi Tamaki and Jun Yoshinaga

Abstract In the earlier chapters of this book, we have shown, with limited evidence, that both the duration of lactational infecundability and time to pregnancy (TTP) may be longer among Japanese couples than among Western couples. Longer TTP can be linked to the relatively low coital frequency and prolonged duration of lactation found in couples and mothers in Japan, as well as to other factors such as long work hours, underweight, and overweight. The relatively longer TTP may be linked to the frequent use of ART among couples in Japan. Efficient use of ART, in terms of who should utilize these technologies and at what time, should be investigated in future studies to better meet couples' needs. We confirm the widely held notions that many Japanese couples continue to rely on unreliable contraception and that induced abortion is common among both married and unmarried women. Conceptions that end in artificial abortions could have a significant impact on fertility trends in Japan if social and other circumstances allowed some of those conceptions to result in live births. It is also important to investigate the biological and sociocultural factors—e.g., exposure to chemical substances, body size, educational level, and working conditions—that may explain variations in TTP and other proximate determinants of fertility. In addition, a model-based approach would enable us to estimate the level of change in each sociocultural factor that would lead to changes in fertility through the modification of proximate determinants. We believe that the accumulation of such data will help us to understand why low levels of fertility persist in Japan.

Keywords Underweight · Overweight · Chemical exposure · Infertility treatment Lactational amenorrhea · Time to pregnancy (TTP) · Japan

4.1 Acquiring Empirical Data on Proximate Determinants of Fertility

Previous studies and the biodemography project show a clear contrast between Japanese and Western populations in terms of proximate determinants of fertility. This contrast suggests that the mechanisms of low fertility trends may differ between Japan and Western populations.

S. Konishi et al., *Biodemography of Fertility in Japan*,
Population Studies of Japan, https://doi.org/10.1007/978-981-10-0176-5_4

For example, Japanese women are characterized by long nursing duration and a high prevalence of breastfeeding, which are suspected to cause longer duration of postpartum amenorrhea compared with mothers in Western settings. Our data indicate that as many as 35% of nursing mothers with 1-year-old children experienced postpartum amenorrhea in 2014 (see Chap. 2), which suggests the possible impact of nursing behavior on secondary infertility. Moreover, a higher proportion of nursing mothers combined with higher ages at childbearing and a higher prevalence of underweight (BMI < 18.5 kg/m^2)—i.e., 21.5% in 20–29-year-olds and 17.7% in 30–39-year-olds in 2013 [1]—among Japanese women of reproductive age might also contribute to the prolonged duration of lactational amenorrhea, taking into account that increased duration of amenorrhea was reported among mothers at higher ages [2] and lower body weights in Bangladesh [2] and in countries in sub-Saharan Africa [3].

Although direct estimates on TTP among Japanese couples are scarce, recent estimates [4] and other indirect data suggest that the wait for conception may be longer for Japanese couples compared to couples in Western settings. We have three reasons for this supposition. First, coital frequency tends to be lower among Japanese couples compared to Western couples, in general, as many as 37% of married Japanese women aged between 30 and 39 years are estimated to live in sexless marriage (Chap. 2). Second, the proportion of ovulatory cycles may be lower for Japanese women due to their underweight status, which can be linked to a higher probability of irregular menstrual cycles (Chap. 2). Third, widespread nursing practice among mothers may lead to reduced fecundability [5], even if they are not experiencing lactational amenorrhea, and thus to secondary infertility. Whether these factors have any significant impact on TTP among Japanese couples remains speculative at this point, and thus further research is needed to determine whether our supposition is correct.

It would also be useful to study the Japanese population to assess whether there is an association between certain proximate determinants—such as proportion of ovulatory cycles and fecundability—and modifiable lifestyle factors, e.g., body size, physical activity, smoking, and alcohol consumption. Although the possible impact of these factors has been evaluated in previous studies overseas [6], it is largely unknown for the Japanese population. Even if the relative effect of such factors is not large, these factors affect a significant proportion of couples in a population and thus may impact fertility. Another merit of examining these factors is that couples can intentionally change them, in contrast to unmodifiable factors, such as age.

Another area of research that we consider worthy of pursuit is the possible effect of chemical exposure on TTP. Although conclusive evidence of a significant negative effect of such exposure on human fecundity has not yet been found, there are studies that suggest a potential impact, as discussed in Chap. 3. We propose that in future studies we should examine the possible impact of chemical exposure on each component of TTP, i.e., the frequency of insemination, length of ovarian cycles, and probability of conception from a single insemination within the fertile period (daily fecundability). To estimate daily fecundability, we need daily data on sexual intercourse, menstrual bleeding, and preferably ovulation accumulated within a study with a prospective design. Additionally, a possible association between chemical exposure and nursing practices is an interesting research topic, given that a cutting-edge study has suggested that chemical exposure might impair lactation [7].

From a more sociocultural perspective, the impact of social factors peculiar to Japanese society, such as working conditions, on each proximate determinant of fertility should be investigated further. Potential topics of interest include the relationships between long working hours of both males and females and factors such as menstrual cycle characteristics, coital frequency, and daily fecundability.

4.2 Interrelationship Between Infertility Treatment and Proximate Determinants of Fertility

Considering that a low frequency of sexual intercourse was commonly found among couples who had experienced ART (Chap. 2), the possible effects of infertility treatment on coital frequency and on the quality of the marital relationship among Japanese couples are worth investigating. Previous studies conducted overseas report that infertility is associated with poor marital adjustment of women and less intercourse satisfaction among men [8], whereas other studies report a beneficial effect of infertility treatment on marital quality [9]. Another study found a negative impact on marital life among women who remained childless after undergoing in vitro fertilization compared with women who gave birth or adopted a child [10]. There are many more studies on this particular topic that target populations abroad, but such studies seem to be quite limited in Japan. Because Japan has the highest number of ART treatment cycles among all countries in the world [11], the possible impact of infertility treatment is expected to be substantial, not only on proximate determinants but also on couples' and families' relationships which would have wider social implications.

In addition to the possible impact of infertility treatment on proximate determinants of fertility, it is important to understand which people are more likely to receive infertility treatment and at what time (i.e., after how many months/years of trying to conceive) and how these factors relate to treatment outcomes. For example, information on duration of trying (right-censored TTP) at the start of medical intervention and data on couples' characteristics (e.g., age, coital frequency, socioeconomic status, reproductive history, and health history) should be collected, as well as information on the type of treatment received and its outcome. From these data, we can examine what factors in addition to age are associated with a higher probability of a live birth, either through natural conception or ART.

4.3 Estimating the Impact of Each Proximate Determinant on Fertility

To understand how all of these biobehavioral and sociocultural factors work to form the observed fertility trend, it would be useful to estimate the relative impact of each factor on each proximate determinant of fertility. One way to estimate the impact of changes in each proximate determinant would be to use a microsimulation model of fertility [12, 13]. However, before deciding on the type of model to use, we need to collect detailed empirical information on each of the proximate determinants and their interrelationships, targeting a population in Japan. We believe that the accumulation of such data will help us to understand why low levels of fertility persist in Japan.

References

1. Ministry of Health, Labour and Welfare. 2016. *Summary report of the National Health and Nutrition Survey 2013 (Heisei 25nen kokumin kenkoeiyo chosa no gaiyo)*. Tokyo: Ministry of Health, Labour and Welfare. (in Japanese).
2. Huffman, Sandra L., Kathleen Ford, Hubert A. Allen Jr., and Peter Streble. 1987. Nutrition and fertility in Bangladesh: Breastfeeding and post partum amenorrhoea. *Population Studies* 41: 447–462.
3. Peng, Y.K., V. Hight-Laukaran, A.E. Peterson, and R. Pérez-Escamilla. 1998. Maternal nutritional status is inversely associated with lactational amenorrhea in Sub-Saharan Africa: Results from demographic and health surveys II and III. *Journal of Nutrition* 128: 1672–1680.
4. Konishi, Shoko, Soyoko Sakata, Mari S. Oba, and Kathleen A. O'Connor. Age and time to pregnancy for the first child among couples in Japan. *The Journal of Population Studies* (in press).
5. John, A.Meredith, Jane A. Menken, and A.K.M. Alauddin Chowdhury. 1987. The effects of breastfeeding and nutrition on fecundability in rural Bangladesh: A hazards-model analysis. *Population Studies* 41: 433–446.
6. Homan, G.F., M. Davies, and R. Norman. 2007. The impact of lifestyle factors on reproductive performance in the general population and those undergoing infertility treatment: A review. *Human Reproduction Update* 13: 209–223.
7. Konkel, Lindsey. 2017. Mother's milk and the environment: Might chemical exposures impair lactation? *Environmental Health Perspectives* 125: A17–A23.
8. Monga, Manoj, Bogdan Alexandrescu, Seth E. Katz, Murray Stein, and Theodore Ganiats. 2004. Impact of infertility on quality of life, marital adjustment, and sexual function. *Urology* 63: 126–130.
9. Schmidt, Lone, Bjørn Holstein, Ulla Christensen, and Jacky Boivin. 2005. Does infertility cause marital benefit? An epidemiological study of 2250 women and men in fertility treatment. *Patient Education and Counseling* 59: 244–251.
10. Leiblum, S.R., A. Aviv, and R. Hamer. 1998. Life after infertility treatment: a long-term investigation of marital and sexual function. *Human Reproduction* 13: 3569–3574.
11. Dyer, S., G.M. Chambers, J. de Mouzon, K.G. Nygren, F. Zegers-Hochschild, R. Mansour, O. Ishihara, M. Banker, and G.D. Adamson. 2016. International Committee for Monitoring Assisted Reproductive Technologies world report: Assisted Reproductive Technology 2008, 2009 and 2010. *Human Reproduction* 31: 1588–1609.

12. Coale, A., and J. Trussell. 1996. The development and use of demographic models. *Population studies* 50: 469–484.
13. Wood, James W., Patricia L. Johnson, and Kenneth L. Campbell. 1985. Demographic and endocrinological aspects of low natural fertility in highland New Guinea. *Journal of Biosocial Science* 17: 59–79.